What we hope they'll be saying in praise of *Summer of the Bats*

If laughter is the best medicine, once you read Summer of the Bats *you won't even need healthcare.*

Barry O.

Summer of the Bats *was so funny, I'd email you a copy myself, but, well, you know . . .*

H.

The top 100% of Americans will love Summer of the Bats.

Bernie

Summer of the Bats *is absolutely the greatest, bestest, funniest, most amazing book ever written. It's going to be a huge success, that I can tell you.*

Donnie T.

Summer of the Bats

Stu Bloom

stu@coastalpenpress.com

For Lynne, Alex and Zack,
the source of love and laughter,
and
my sweet girl, Molly

That book was made by Mr. Mark Twain, and he told the truth, mainly. There was things which he stretched, but mainly he told the truth.

The Adventures of Huckleberry Finn
Mark Twain

I.

It was just so fucking hot.

Slow-motion hot. Shoulders heavy under the weight of a blazing sun, feet dragging through molten molasses. The heat that didn't weigh you down crawled up your legs, up through the soles of your shoes. The news blared admonitions to keep hydrated. You squinted through the hot, white sunshine, through the waves wiggling above the blacktop. You sucked in hot air, searched for the slightest hint of a breeze. An unwelcome stop on the road to hell.

We were having the inside of the house painted.

The old house in Connecticut. Charming.

I remembered the realtor walking us through the house when we first saw it. I had commented on the lack of central air-conditioning. In accordance with the Realtor's Bible, she dismissed the negative: It's in the woods. You're under the trees, lots of shade—just a couple of warm days in August. You don't even need air-conditioning.

Now we sat in the family room, glued to the leather couch by the heat, the air still and stifling. Laura sat with a bag of ice on her head, hand cupped over her mouth and nose, futile defense against the paint fumes. Her favorite month of the year is January. She was in a very good mood.

Number one son, Jason, came into the room with a canvas bag slung over his shoulder. He was getting ready to leave, his weekend visit cut short by the painting.

Hey, he asked off-handedly as he said his good-byes and prepared to depart, what's with all those bats that came flying out of the house last night?

Bats? Bats? Are you kidding? What kind of bats? Laura was clearly taken aback.

Bats. Lots of them. They flew right out from under the roof and into the woods. Like millions of them. Didn't you know there were bats? You know, bats are good.

My god. Bats?

It was years ago, long before we knew anything about bats, that we took the big leap. Moved to Connecticut from The City. Manhattan. Where you got fruit from the Korean green grocer on the corner, pizza up the block, Chinese food from the menus shoved under the door. If there was no hot water, you called the Super. If the dryer wasn't working, you called the Super. If the toilet was running, you called the Super. As long as you took care of the Super at Christmastime, life was simple. The only brushes with wildlife were the pigeons in the park, the deeply filed away and largely ignored sense that rats ruled the city from somewhere beneath the subway tracks, and a constant vigilance to keep the kitchen scrupulously clean and free of cockroaches. Our own pest-avoidance strategy included a pantry stocked with bundles of wrapped food secured with rubber bands, Russian doll–like layers of plastic bags inside plastic bags inside plastic bags. With the meticulous bug-proofing protocol, it took ten minutes to get a lousy pistachio and another ten to put the package back. I came to rely solely on refrigerated foods.

On that moving day years ago, three very big men—buildings with legs—unloaded and placed our furniture in the new house, and then we watched with a touch of sadness as the moving van pulled away, winding back up the long lane, and disappearing into the woods, retracing its route to the main road and a return to civilization. Laura and I stood in our new driveway as night fell. It was dark. So dark. Really dark. It was black. You couldn't see your hand in front of your face.

Jeez. I peered through the darkness, looking for any slight movement, trying to make out the shadowy image of my wife. Where do you get ice cream in a place like this?

Ice cream? Forget ice cream. Do you think there are bears?

Bears?

Yes, bears. Do you think there are bears? I think I read about bears.

There are no bears.

Oh yeah? How do you know? All of a sudden you're an expert on mammoth man-eating mammals? I think there are bears here. I think this is where bears live.

There are no bears. This is where we live.

Well, there better not be bears. First sign of a bear, I'm outta here.

Let's go inside.

Why? You think there are bears?

We've got to get some lights out here. It's really dark.

Yeah. We want to make sure the bears can find us.

Hey, if anything, lights will keep the bears away.

Keep the bears away? So you *do* think there are bears! I knew it.

There are no bears. Enough with the bears. Let's get inside.

It was early August when we moved in. Two full acres set in the woods with a big clearing for the house. Lots of grass, well, lots of green. We had made the life passage from Manhattan apartment dwellers to country squires.

That first Saturday morning, I stepped out onto the back deck and took in the property, preening with the satisfaction of ownership. The sky was blue; the trees were green; the woods were beautiful. If I'd worn suspenders, I'd have hooked my thumbs in them. I was a land baron. I folded my arms across my chest, nodded in approval and surveyed the grounds with more than a hint of smugness. Stood there, nodding, surveying, surveying, nodding.

Damn, I thought, we're going to need a lawn mower. A serious lawn mower.

Hey, Jason, I called. Since the day we moved in he'd been holed up in his new room, lamenting the exodus from The City. Hey, Jason, I called again, come on down here.

No response. He was royally pissed off. We'd dragged him away from his friends, his school, his local haunts, his independence, to this hellhole on earth where you needed a car to get anywhere, where no one knew how to talk or dress, where you couldn't even find a decent slice of pizza. How do you live in a place without a subway? It sucked. It sucked big time. It sucked the soul right out of him.

Hey, Jason, come on, let's take a ride, I called.

No way was he coming down. I went up. Knocked on the door.

Go away.

I went in.

He was curled up in a corner, fetal position, listening to the sound track of *Les Misérables*.

What? More a demand than a question.

Come on, take a ride with me.

Where? What for? He spoke but didn't move.

To get a lawn mower.

For what?

To mow the lawn. We need to mow the lawn. We need a lawn mower to mow the lawn.

In The City, they don't have lawns.

But here we do.

Whose fault is that?

The grass gods. Come on, take a ride with me. It'll be fun.

That's what you call fun now? Getting a lawn mower?
That's fun?

Come on, don't just lie here listening to this stuff. It's
depressing.

I like it.

This is what you call fun? *Les Misérables*? A mournful
voice was wailing about bringing someone home. No doubt
Jason yearned for someone to bring him home.

It reminds me of New York.

It takes place in Paris.

At least they don't have lawn mowers.

Jason was at that awkward, junior high age when we
departed The City for points north. As a young teenager
testing limits, nearly everything was a battle. He had a long
list of grievances and arguments as to why The City was
better than, well, anywhere. On the other hand, our younger,
elementary aged son Matt took to our new digs like a fish to
water or, in his case, like a kid to dirt. He loved having a big
yard, happy to run wild for the sole purpose of falling to the
ground giggling. Often times, Laura would be watching him
and then mutter, to no one in particular, It's a shame he's
going to turn into a teenager someday.

The salesman was wearing a sky-blue shirt with sharply creased short sleeves that dwarfed a meek pair of biceps. His face was polished and extended right up through a freckled head beneath a wispy comb-over of disappearing red hair. The brown name badge over the shirt pocket said Arnold.

Hey there, can I help you? Whattchalookin' for?

A lawn mower.

Well, whattaya need?

A lawn mower?

No, I mean you got different kinds for different jobs. What do you need?

To mow the lawn.

All right. Well, how big is the lawn? You think you need a rider?

Big.

How big?

I don't know. Big. It's a big lawn. It's smaller in the front, but it's bigger in the back.

Big—like a field? Like for a tractor? Where do you live?

I told him.

Oh, two-acre zoning?

Yeah, I brightened. Two-acre zoning. I knew the answer from the whole real estate thing. I felt like I'd just won a round on *Jeopardy*.

So, what's the deal with this baby? I put my macho on and pointed to a machine at the end of a long double row of lawn mowers. What can I do to put you in this baby today? I said grinning.

Huh?

Arnie didn't like my choice. There wasn't anything Arnie didn't know about lawn mowers, and he let me know it. He talked horsepower, drivetrains, RPMs, rotary blades. He talked and talked and pointed and talked. I gave up. I could see his mouth moving, and I could sense a series of syllables, but I had absolutely no comprehension of the stream of lawn-mowerese that was spilling forth.

As my eyelids began to droop, I yanked my head up and said, I'll take the red one.

Arnie's face dropped. In a voice rich with second-guessing, he recited all the features that my choice was missing—autowalk, self-propelled drive; super-duper, extra-hardened, tungsten-tempered steel blades; a remote autostarting ignition-ease watsamafrass; grass whispering; semi-self-lubricating; four-wheel drive; iPhone connection;

refrigerated refreshment compartment; six preset radio stations; voice-activated Bluetooth integration . . .

I liked the red one. It looked like the lawn mower we had when I was a kid.

What the heck, I thought, I'm not even going to be the one mowing the lawn—Jason is.

Later that afternoon, after a long, loud and intellectually stimulating debate that featured razor-sharp sarcasm, foot stomping and outright threats, Jason cheerfully agreed to perform his fair share of the chores. He would mow the lawn.

Anyway, as he delicately put it, at least it's something to do in this shit hole of a town.

I knew he'd come around.

Jason, recent Manhattan prep schooler, dweller of high rises, and adroit navigator of busses and subways, emerged from the solitude of his room. On this excessively warm August Sunday morning, he was ready to mow the lawn.

He was wearing khaki pants, a blue oxford, long-sleeve, button-down shirt, and cordovan loafers.

It was a pretty June day, those years ago, when we agreed to buy the house. It seemed perfect. A nice, reasonably sized house for our family, nestled down a quiet, winding, rolling private lane among a few similar houses that dotted the woods in the cute, closely knit Connecticut town of Littleton.

The most important thing about house hunting is understanding real estate speak. Familiarity with real estate vocabulary can save you lots of time and money. A quick primer:

Cozy means *small.*

Cute means *small.*

Perfect for a young family means *small.*

A great starter home means *small.*

Charming means *small.*

Loaded with charm means *old.*

Full of character means *old.*

Needs some TLC means *really old.*

A fixer-upper means *Do you own a backhoe?*

Of course, no amount of conversational facility with real estate speak can prepare you for when your realtor pulls up to show you a house that sits across from a cemetery and says, Now *this* is a really quiet neighborhood.

Swear to god.

The negotiations didn't amount to much. Our broker went back and forth on the phone with the seller's agent even as we toured other houses. We traded figures edging toward a compromise, but progress was beginning to slow. Finally, our realtor gave us a price and said the seller would include the pool table in the basement and the snowblower in the garage, which, apparently, they weren't going to need in their new home in Malibu.

Look, I said. Here's my final price, and I don't want the pool table, and I don't want the snowblower. That's it.

The offer was accepted.

I was an idiot.

Private lane means the town has no responsibility for road maintenance, no snowplowing. Since our very first December in the house I've wished I'd taken that snowblower—every time Laura and I shovel the driveway, trudge up the lane with heavy buckets of salt to scatter over the roadbed like chicken feed, hands frozen, slipping down the hill, backs aching. We call ourselves the road crew.

Look, I don't want the snowblower, I hear myself saying over and over again.

On the bright side, I still don't play pool.

Keeping the lawn mowed was only the beginning. Our house sits in what is essentially a clearing in the woods. We're engaged in a perpetual battle to fight back the forest from encroaching onto our relatively small patch of civilization.

For years, we weeded, trimmed, pulled and dug; we spread and smoothed; we contoured and edged. Nothing worked. The woods kept coming.

One hot afternoon, I looked up from my digging to see Laura atop our hill in full Lyme disease defense attire: pants tucked into socks into work boots, long-sleeve shirt and gloves, hair wrapped in a scarf, and a beekeeper's veil over her head. She was pulling at the ever-advancing vegetation, weeding away, tilting at windmills. Drops of sweat fell from her face as if she'd just emerged from a swim. We were both dirty, exhausted, aching and ineffective. She got up from her knees for a moment, arched her back to relieve the stiffness and looked down the hill at me.

Truly, if looks could kill. Land baron, my ass.

The beat-back-the-woods battle was relentless. The more we pulled and trimmed and pruned, the more the growth advanced undaunted.

There must be some kind of tool, I thought. Some kind of weapon.

Off to Home-Is-Us, the local big-box home fix-it center that sells everything you could possibly need for renovation, fabrication and aggravation. I wandered the aisles, not knowing exactly what I was looking for but sure I'd know it when I saw it.

There. A sickle. A cutting blade where I could let loose a warrior's battle cry as I dove into the underbrush, hacking away, fighting back the woods with my own two hands.

Back at the house, I charged into the overgrowth, whipsawing back and forth, slicing through the brush. I was a wild man. I swung that blade until it felt like my arms were going to fly off. Must've been a good three or four minutes. But I was making progress. There was a big cleared spot maybe five feet in diameter. I had cleared the brush. In three or four years, I'd have my property back.

That night the rain came. Torrents. It was actually quite refreshing. We enjoyed it.

The next morning you could see the mudslide trail running down the hill across the back lawn. In clearing the circle of brush, I'd freed the mud. The Great Mud Emancipator. It was a lesson in land management, in erosion control. Once I cleared the land, I would need something to hold it in place.

It was a vexing puzzle until one afternoon when I was driving past a nearby house. I saw it. A circle on the ground surrounding a large tree in the center of the front lawn. Heavenly music swelled through the car as enlightenment descended upon my entire being. I was bathed in the light of emerging wisdom. There, before me, was one of the great secrets of life, the solution to any problem, the cure for all our ills—that could feed the hungry, put an end to poverty, and bring peace to all the world.

Wood chips.

There's hardly a problem you can't solve with wood chips. Stop the erosion, mulch the garden, fill in the path, border the driveway, edge the trees. Wood chips. I had them brought in by the truckload. Dumped piles on the driveway. Bought three wheelbarrows and three shovels. Set up Laura and the kids in an assembly line and moved those wood chips everywhere. By the time we were finished, there wasn't an empty spot on the property that wasn't covered in wood chips.

The land-reclamation project wasn't our only problem. There were lots of issues to deal with, each with its own expert. A continuous parade of characters streamed in and out of our house, in and out of our lives. It was like a sitcom, with an unending lineup of secondary players and celebrity guests moving through our world. There was the trash guy, the water-pump guy, the oil guy, the electrician, the painter, the exterminator, the landscaper, the lawn-maintenance guy (different from the landscaper), the lawn-restoration guy (different from the lawn-maintenance guy and the landscaper), the chimney sweep (yes, chimney sweep), the plumber, the handyman, the recycling guy (same company as the trash guy, different guy), the tree guy, the floor guy, the window guy, the curtain-hanging guy. Several guys who I had no idea what they did. It was endless.

One of the great things about the house was the fireplace—a real, working, wood-burning fireplace. I loved it. That first year in the house I couldn't wait for those autumn afternoons of football, beer, chips, and a crackling fire. The more sophisticated me, which existed only in some far-off erudite fantasyland, envisioned snowy winter evenings, a glass of wine, a good book, and sitting by the fire. I planned to reread (uh, read), the *Complete Works of Shakespeare*, *War and Peace*, and several volumes of Robert Frost poems. I made a mental note to pick up a couple of cardigan sweaters. I loved that we had a fireplace, and I couldn't wait to use it.

It was a nice crisp September afternoon that first autumn in the house. I was driving down the lane on the way home when I saw one of my neighbors out on his property, brandishing a chain saw, cutting freshly downed tree trunks into smaller pieces, leaving a bunch of fat logs scattered about the lawn. I slowed to wave in greeting, and he motioned me over. The toasted scent of freshly cut wood hung in the air.

Hey, how you doing?

Great. I see you're playing lumberjack for the day.

Yeah, just trying to get a little land cleared, let in a little more light.

Looking good.

Well, you want to take some for firewood?

Firewood? Yeah! Are you sure? Hey, sure, I'll buy some from you.

No, no. Take what you want. Really. Here, I'll help you load it.

You sure?

Yeah, of course. Come on.

I popped the trunk, and we started loading some logs.

Here, take the ones cut to size, he pointed to a stack of smaller cut pieces.

Perfect for my fire, I thought.

I gathered up a few logs in my arms and piled them into the trunk.

Hey, that's great. Thanks. Thanks a lot. That's great.

No, no, he said, take some more. Fill up the trunk.

Wow, that's awfully generous.

I didn't want to be a pig about the whole thing.

Hey, that's great, really, I said. You sure I can't pay you something? That's an awful lot of wood.

No, not at all, he smiled. Grab what you can.

I filled the trunk, thanked him again and continued down the lane into our driveway. It wasn't cold at all, but I was pretty excited about building a fire.

Hey, Laur-o, I yelled, getting out of the car. We're going to make a fire!

I filled my arms with a bundle of logs from the trunk and, leaving the rest behind, manipulated my way through the garage door and into the family room. I felt the first log slipping, shifted my weight to keep it from falling, and lost control of the whole bunch. They went crashing down onto the floor. The newly finished hardwood floor. One log landed on my foot.

What was that? Laura said as she came into the room. What are you doing? You're going to kill yourself—and ruin the floor. Come on, we just had the floor guy here.

Hey, it's a hardwood floor, I smiled, grimacing just a little.

What is all this, anyway?

I'm going to make a fire. We're going to have a fire in our fireplace. It's gonna be great. Best thing yet.

Oh, wow! Do you know how it works? Do you know how to make a fire?

What are you talking about, how it works? It's a fireplace. You put wood in it. You light a match. You got fire.

Maybe we can call someone. Maybe you can get someone to show you how, she said with a bit of genuine concern and a healthy dose of skepticism.

What do you mean, call someone? There's nothing to it. Come on, elementary physics. Heat, fuel, oxygen. Fire.

She didn't look convinced. She always wanted to call someone.

Hey—I can light a fire. Hell, I was a Webelo.

OK. It will be nice in the winter. She sat down on the couch to watch.

I made a pile of logs at the bottom of the fireplace. I crisscrossed them, I explained, so that the air would circulate. That will make a better fire. Nice and lively, I said. (Nice and lively?)

OK, ready. Gimme a match.

A match? I don't have a match.

There must be matches around here somewhere.

Why? Why must there be matches around here somewhere?

It's a common household item. This is a household. Where the hell are the matches?

What matches?

Matches! We've gotta have matches around here somewhere.

No one smokes in this house.

Yeah, but what if we need a match for something.

Like what?

Like for lighting the fire!

I catch either of those boys smoking, I'll kill them. Fine. I'll get some matches.

We sat there for a few moments. Well, she sat. I stood there looking at my lifeless pile of logs in the fireplace.

Well?

Well, what?

Well, I thought you were going to get some matches.

What? Now? You want me to go now, in the middle of everything? I'll get them when I go to the store.

And when will that be?

Tuesday. I go shopping Tuesday.

Tuesday? What good is Tuesday? I want to light the fire now!

Hey, don't jump at me just because you don't have matches. And stop getting all excited. We'll have a fire next weekend. It'll be fun. We'll roast marshmallows.

What? This isn't a marshmallow fire. This is a glass of wine, a good book, sit-by-the kind of fire. We're not having a weenie roast here.

Well, you do what you want. I want to finish the cabinets.

She was always putting shelving paper in cabinets. I never knew what happened to the old shelving paper. I don't even know why cabinets need shelving paper, but it was a never-ending project.

I wanted a fire now. Today. I had a car full of firewood and a fireplace just waiting to be fired up. I was fired up. My toe was starting to swell up.

Got back in the car and drove to the grocery—Jimmy's—a little store in the little town next to ours. Local high school kids at the registers along with one old crone who'd probably always been there. Always. Like they had built the store around her. I'd been stopping into Jimmy's most mornings for a bagel and coffee. The old crone would be at the register, paging through the newspaper, head down, discouraging patrons. Sometimes she'd be texting on her phone or, clipboard in hand, self-importantly surveying the candy racks or checking the fluid levels on the coffee urns. Anything to avoid dealing with an actual customer. Even though I sometimes ended up in her checkout lane, I didn't know her, didn't speak with her. I was a little afraid of her. Her name was Doreen. As a sign of affection, everyone called her Doreen.

Hi, I said brightly. I need some matches. Doreen didn't look up from her paper but slid her hand under the counter and tossed a book of matches at me.

Here.

No. I need a full box, you know, a full box of matches.

I couldn't ever remember buying matches.

Over there, she said, tilting her head toward the front of the store. I couldn't tell where she was pointing, and I was afraid to ask, so I wandered over to the shelves and began scanning hopefully. By all outward appearances, I was a discriminating buyer of toilet scrub brushes and Handi Wipes.

To the left, I heard her growl.

Yeah, yeah, I got it. I just wanted to see something, relieved at having spotted the matches. All right. At least now we were fixed for matches. Check that off the old list.

I was glad to be out of there. Back to my fire. My toe hurt.

OK. The wood was stacked in the fireplace. I had my matches. We were ready to go.

I struck a match and bent down, holding it to the underside of a log. The futility was evident immediately. Well, almost immediately. I tried a couple more matches, and then a couple more, holding the last to the bark, figuring it would more easily catch flame. Nothing doing.

Oh, what an idiot, I thought, chuckling to myself, as if patiently and patronizingly assessing the simple stupidity of someone else. Kindling. I need some kindling.

Newspaper. I could use newspaper.

Hey, Laura, I called out. Where do we keep the old newspapers?

What? Came a reply from somewhere not too far away. She was in the vicinity.

Newspapers. I need some old newspapers. Where do we keep the old newspapers?

She came into the family room, hugging a basket of laundry.

What?

I was getting exasperated. Why didn't she know what I wanted without me having to ask?

Newspapers. I need some old newspapers to start the fire. Where do we keep the old newspapers?

We don't keep old newspapers.

What do you mean?

What do you mean, what do I mean? We don't keep old newspapers. They're old. They're done. She enunciated one word at a time: They're. Not. News. Any. More.

She smiled, appreciating her own wit.

It's old news. She was enjoying this.

Come on, I said, what do we do with the old newspapers?

I tie them up in a bundle and put them out in the recycling bin for the recycling guy.

We have a recycling guy?

He comes on Fridays.

Today is Saturday.

Yes.

Then . . .

They're gone.

Did you read the paper today? I asked with a timid trace of hope.

No.

Do we have today's paper?

I don't have it. Didn't you take the paper with you when you went for coffee this morning?

Yeah.

Well then . . .

I left it at Dandy Donuts.

What were you doing at Dandy Donuts?

Having coffee.

And donuts? Those greasy donuts?

No, no. They have muffins too. I have the muffins.

How many muffins?

A muffin.

Well, you shouldn't be eating those donuts. They're nothing but sugar.

I'm not eating donuts. I like the coffee.

I'm just saying.

OK. So we don't have any newspapers?

No. Our newspaper is at Dandy Donuts, with your greasy donuts.

What else do we have that I can use?

Use for what?

To light the fire!

I don't know. Is there such a thing as a fire lighter?

Well, we must have some kind of paper around here. Some kind of paper we don't need.

She disappeared for a minute and came back to hand me a bunch of orange papers stapled together.

What's this?

The PTA newsletter. I already read it.

I took the newsletter and, wanting to preserve my supply of kindling, tore off the first page and rolled it up. I lit one end and held it to a log. The flame quickly travelled along the paper tube, rapidly reducing it to ash. I made adjustments to keep the flame in contact with the log without burning myself. Futile.

It doesn't look like it's working, Laura assessed. Maybe you can call someone.

God, my foot hurt.

It just needs more kindling, that's all.

I took apart the newsletter pages and tucked them into spaces among the stacked logs. Lit the papers, watched them flare up, fizzle out and turn to nothing. The logs remained cold and distant, untouched by heat or emotion.

Let's do the fire next weekend, Laura said brightly. Maybe during the week you can ask someone.

Just never mind. I'll figure this out.

I needed like a real whole damn newspaper. They have newspapers at Jimmy's.

Doreen was checking out the candy racks, clipboard in hand, taking care of business. Got my newspaper. In. Out.

Back at the fireplace, I pulled all the logs out, then put a section of the newspaper at the bottom. The Arts. Just as well. I put some logs on top of the paper, then another layer of paper, then more logs, then more paper. I had an unruly stack of logs with paper sticking out all over the place. One match, I thought, and we're going to have a conflagration.

I set a match to the paper at a few different spots. What the hell, I was plenty fixed for matches. The paper caught fire and raised a big flame. Ha! Then the room started filling up with smoke. I mean real smoke.

What the— The smoke was pouring out of the fireplace. Up the chimney, I urged. Go up the chimney!

But it didn't work. I just stood there, not knowing what to do and hoping to god that Laura was nowhere close by. Our new house was going to go up in flames. It crossed my mind that this town might not even have a fire department.

And then the smoke alarm started screaming. Wild, ear-piercing, icepick-through-your-scull, screaming beeping. I waved my hands frantically to try to dissipate the smoke, but the alarm wouldn't quit. It was alarming! The dog started barking. The alarm kept screaming.

What's going on?! Laura came running into the room.

The smoke alarm. The smoke. I shouted as if in a windstorm.

The noise was overwhelming.

Are we on fire? Call 911! Call 911!

No! No! It's the smoke from the fireplace. I was shouting, my hands pressed to my ears.

I started jumping up and down, flailing uselessly at the smoke alarm on the ceiling. Couldn't reach it.

A broom, I shouted. Get me a broom! I was jumping like I was on a pogo stick. Oh my god! The noise, the noise! Get me a broom!

Here, here, she yelled, handing me a broom, whereupon I started swinging the broom ineffectually at the screaming smoke alarm, which, I was sure, began interspersing a mocking laugh between the piercing beeps.

Laura watched this exhibition of derring-do and then took things into her own hands.

Out of the way, she directed, and pulled a chair under the shrieking alarm, climbed up and pushed the button.

The blessed silence.

I stood down with my broom.

What are you doing? Burning down the house? She was really angry. What's with all this smoke?

I was trying to get the fire started, I said sheepishly.

Well, can you please keep the house in one piece! Do you think maybe now you can ask someone how to do this?

Meanwhile, nearly as quickly as the flames started, they vanished, leaving behind only a residue of burnt paper and a lingering acidic fog. I waved away the smoke and stared into the cold, lifeless fireplace. The stack of logs sat untouched. Paper ashes fluttered silently to rest.

Why didn't the smoke go up the chimney? Maybe something was stuck up there. Something was blocking it. I didn't really want to look too closely—what if it was a dead animal or something? I gingerly stuck my head into the fireplace and looked up. There was a handle. I pulled on it. Nothing. I pushed it. It opened and caught on some teeth. A vent of some kind. Hmm, maybe this vent should be open.

Despite the fracas, or maybe because of it, I was determined. More paper, more logs, paper, logs, paper, logs. And light it. The flame flared up. No smoke. Up through the chimney it went. Aha! Call someone, my ass.

But the flames quickly died again. No fire. Just ashes from the newspaper. Logs unscorched and defiant.

How's it going? She was checking on me, making sure I was still in one piece.

Not going yet.

What do you think's the matter?

Nothing's the matter.

Well, what's with the fire? she asked kindly. I recognized her pity face.

I had no answer. I stared into the fireplace. There was nowhere else to look.

I can't get the logs to light.

Why not?

Again, no answer.

Maybe you need some sticks.

Huh? What?

Maybe you need some sticks. You know, little sticks. You light those, they start the fire, then the logs catch on fire. Little sticks.

We can try it, I guess.

She left the room and left me to my fire.

Of course, I thought, little sticks. Real kindling!

I limped out to the yard, to the edge of the woods. I collected twigs, sticks. They were everywhere. Plenty. In just a couple of minutes my arms were full, couldn't hold any more. I dropped the whole bunch to the ground and went looking for a bucket. Couldn't find a bucket. Ran, er, limped inside and got a towel. Tried to pick one she wouldn't miss. Pulled out a towel and then hurried, as best as my bulbous toe would carry me, back out to my bunch of sticks. I lay the towel on the ground and piled on the sticks, then grabbed a bunch more, filled the towel, wrapped it up, threw the bundle over my shoulder, hobo-like, and ran, er, hobbled, inside. Very excited.

I had sticks. Little sticks, medium sticks, big sticks. I pulled the logs out of the fireplace and built a bed of sticks, excuse me, kindling, on the floor of the fireplace, then stacked the logs on top.

I rolled up one of my last pieces of newspaper and lit it, setting the paper to the twigs. A couple of the small sticks caught fire. A weak flame, but they were on fire, and they were staying lit.

Ha! We were on our way.

The slight flame moved through the pile of sticks. There was something going on down there. Yeah! I shouted with a fist pump. We had fire!

Shit.

The flames started fizzling out, and still the logs hadn't caught fire. Some of the sticks were turning to glowing embers. I got down on my hands and knees and started blowing on them. It worked! A flame reappeared. The flames died out in another part of the pile, and I blew on those. The flames sprouted back. Again they died, and I blew some more. Blew some more.

Still, none of the logs caught fire. Down on my hands and knees, I blew some more. Kept blowing. I blew at the flames, trying to get the fire to rise in a blaze. It kinda sorta worked. The flames popped up. One briefly lit a corner of a log but died out quickly. I was onto something. I was down on the floor, leaning into the fireplace, head tilted to the side and blowing for all my life. When the flames shot up, I blew some more, trying to urge the flames onto the logs. Every time the flame from a section of sticks died out, I blew some more. A few of the logs caught a flame and just kind of sizzled there. No flame, but a lit end and smoke. I huffed and I puffed and I blew some more.

I was out of breath. Dizzy. I flopped back on the floor. Tried to catch my breath. Tried to make the room stop spinning.

I sucked it up.

I got down on my hands and knees and blew some more while there was still a lingering chance of raising the flames.

I blew and blew. I blew until it was hardly worth blowing. My head grew light. My blowing grew lighter. I was running out of steam. Out of breath. Out of everything. I gave up.

Resigned, I watched the last of the little flames die out, turn cold, turn to nothing. A sad sight. I grabbed a corner of the couch to steady myself, to make the room slow down. I collapsed to the floor and stared at the ceiling.

Maybe I could call someone.

The next day I was driving up the lane when I passed my lumberjack neighbor. He was out stacking more logs.

Hey, I called, lowering the window. How's it going?

Goin' good. Want some more wood? He smiled and nodded toward the stack.

Nah. I'll tell you the truth. I couldn't get them to light yesterday. Nothing but a little smoke. Man, I chuckled, I was like a human bellows, blowing and blowing, trying to get that fire started. Nearly passed out. Maybe there's something wrong with the fireplace.

What? You tried to burn that wood yesterday?

Yeah, sure.

Nah, you can't do that. That's fresh-cut wood. You can't burn that until next year. You need seasoned wood to burn now.

Seasoned wood?

Sure.

You mean I got to salt the wood?

He couldn't answer right away, trying to hold back the laugh.

No, ha ha. Wood has to dry out before you can use it for a fire. You got to age it for about a year. That wood is freshly cut—won't do anything but sit there and smoke. You can blow on it all you want, not going to have any real fire.

Sure won't, I thought.

Well, that's what happens when you bring the city boy to the country, I chuckled.

Jeez, the guy thinks I'm a total idiot.

At home that evening, I sat brooding, staring at the fireplace, the fresh logs still piled inside, cold and idle, barely singed, mocking me. OK. So I need old wood.

Out and about the next Saturday, I was gassing up the car and saw the sign. Firewood. There it was, piled in little bundles, wrapped in plastic. Kiln Dried. Seasoned Firewood.

I bought two bundles—one for today, one for tomorrow. An early autumn weekend by the fire. Joy. My toe hardly hurt anymore. Ha. Filled the tank and threw the bundles of wood into the trunk. Done. I am going to have a fire today, damn it. Right now.

Hey! Look at this. I got firewood.

Laura looked puzzled.

You bought firewood? What about all that wood you brought home last week?

Tell you later. Right now, I'm going to light a fire. Pour a glass of wine, maybe a little cheese; just going to relax by my fire.

Wine? It's ten thirty in the morning.

Oh.

Did you get the cleanser?

Huh?

The tile cleaner. Remember, I asked you to pick up tile cleaner since you were going out.

No. I forgot.

You forgot?

Yeah, I forgot.

How could you forget?

How?

Yeah, how?

I just forgot. I was all excited about the firewood.

Well then, now I have to go out to the store. Do you need anything?

Nope. When you get back, we'll have a fire.

When I get back, I want to work on that tile upstairs.

You can do that anytime. Today we're having a fire.

And then I want to put shelving paper in the linen closet.

It was early, I had to admit. What kind of fireside atmosphere was there that early on a Saturday? Wine at ten thirty in the morning? Hell, I'd just barely finished my coffee.

I sighed. OK, the fire would have to wait until later. I still had my two bundles of wood. I just needed to kill some time.

Home-Is-Us scares me. Cars in the parking lot weaving every which way, panel trucks and oversized SUVs backing out of parking spaces without so much as a glance behind. Every time you think there's an empty spot, there's some little car squeezed in next to a pickup truck that's blocking the view. People in baggy carpenter pants and paint-spattered overalls are pushing big orange carts with sheets of aluminum siding, chimney bricks and barn doors sticking out all over. They can't see over the pile of building materials, and they load things into the trucks and then drive off to secret construction sites where they're building small empires on a budget.

Inside, heavy roving machines beep incessantly, trolling the aisles for innocent victims to run over, leaving the blood-splattered remains in their wake like big orange robo-dinosaurs depositing their waste behind them.

I wander along the main strip at the front of the store, looking for the aisle of bathroom stuff. I need new handles for our bathroom cabinets. I've got a small sample in my hand, one of the old handles I removed from the cabinet, a demonstration of my mechanical prowess and skill with tools. Finally, I see a wide aisle lined with bathroom fixtures: a row of toilets along the second-tier shelf above, tilted as if to pour water on the passing customers; a long row of threatening thrones; single-sink vanities, double-sink vanities, vanities without sinks, vanities without tops and vanity tops; shower stalls; sinks; bathtubs. I ambled up and down that aisle three times. It was full of lots of big things. Things that require the ability to do stuff, to put things together, to bond, to seal, to connect, to know how things work, to hammer, to saw, to mount, to tighten, to fit. Stuff. Nowhere do I see the little handles I need.

Two guys in orange aprons come walking down the aisle deep in conversation. I wave my little handle at them, with a maybe-you-can-help-me gesture and a grin. They split up to pass by me on either side and continue talking. They're gone.

Here comes another Home-Is-Us–aproned woman.

Maybe you can help me?

What do you need?

I'm looking for bathroom cabinet handles. Like this one.

I don't know anything about that. Let me get you someone.

OK.

OK.

She disappeared. I waited. And waited. And waited. Deep down, I knew no one was coming, but still, I waited some more. I half expected that a disembodied voice would somehow surround me saying, *Your handle is very important to us. All our handle persons are busy helping other customers. Please wait here in the aisle like a moron, and the next available handle person will be with you shortly*, and then hum the theme from *Titanic*.

There I stood in Home-Is-Us wasteland, frightened, friendless, alone. Lost in acres of building materials amid purposeful, striding workmen with places to go, stuff to do, things to fix, palaces to build. Guys who did stuff. I sucked it up. Resolute, and with a burst of courage, I set out on my own again.

I found a wide aisle stacked with bathroom cabinets. Must be getting close. A shiver of optimism rushed through my body. Where there are bathroom cabinets, there are sure to be bathroom cabinet handles, right? I scoured the shelves of big things. Craned my neck to see the upper shelves, stooped to see the lower shelves. Nothing. I scanned the horizon hopefully, searching for an orange apron.

Aha! I spotted one. I didn't want to move too quickly; afraid I'd startle him and scare him off. He was with another customer, pointing out stuff on the shelves, answering questions. I bided my time. I'd found a live one, and I wasn't going anywhere. He answered a lot of questions. A lot of questions. What else could this woman possibly want to know? I swear they were now moving onto theories of quantum mechanics. I assumed the Mars flight she was apparently planning was not going to take off for at least several months, and so I grew more impatient. I began making forced guttural sounds that devolved into a hacking cough. Finally, the colloquy ended. I quietly approached the orange guy, slowly, gingerly—a supplicant. I extended my bathroom handle in the palm of my open hand, facing up so as not to spook him.

I'm looking for replacement handles for my bathroom cabinets, I said, nodding toward my handy handle.

I'm in plumbing.

I had no response.

Um, sorry?

I'm in plumbing. You need hardware.

Hardware?

Aisle 16, he pointed over his shoulder with his thumb.

It was past lunchtime. I was going to starve to death in the plumbing aisle at Home-Is-Us.

Having decided not to wait for the bus, I set out on a moderate hike to aisle 16, wincing at the loud beeps and dodging a barrage of orange robo-dinosaurs along the way. Aisle 16 was loaded top to bottom with all kinds of thingamajigs and doodads. My heart fluttered. There was hope.

An orange apron was moving along the aisle, slowly, sideways, eyes scanning the upper shelves, then the eye-level shelves, then the lower shelves as he moved back and forth. He was followed closely by a white-haired do-it-yourselfer who kept saying, See? See? There aren't any here.

I don't see any.

I told you. There aren't any here. Where would they be?

I don't know. I don't see any.

Yeah. You don't see any because there aren't any here.

No, I don't see any.

Where else might they be?

I don't know. I don't see any here.

I know; they're not here. Where else could they be?

They would be here, but I don't see any.

Like backup dancers, we all stepped to the side to allow a beeping orange dinosaur to pass. I looked down to make sure my toes were still in place, then looked up and they were gone—the customer and orange guy, not my toes. The DIYer stomped off one way, the orange apron headed in another. I ran to catch up to the apron, waving my cabinet handle.

I need some replacements for these, I gasped, just a little out of breath. I held up the handle to show him.

Whatcha lookin' for?

These, I nodded to the handle in my hand again. I need to replace these. I need new handles for my bathroom cabinets.

Pulls.

Huh?

Pulls. You're looking for pulls.

Huh?

Pulls.

It wasn't clear how long this was going to go on. I don't understand. What do you mean?

Pulls. They're called pulls. You're looking for cabinet pulls.

OK, pulls. I need new pulls.

Sure. Whaddaya lookin' for?

I was out of explanations, just looked back and forth from my handle (I mean pull) to him. After a few moments, I found my voice.

I need these. I looked to my hand again and nodded for emphasis. I need to replace these on my bathroom cabinets.

Yeah. Wood, plastic, brass, chrome, knobs, pulls? They're all along these shelves here. He waved a hand. If you tell me what you're looking for, I can show you.

There was talk of finishes, holes, drawers, doors. It was all a blur. I bought some, secure in the knowledge that they were the wrong thing.

Finally back at home, I was all excited. It was late enough in the day for my fire, a midafternoon fire. I envisioned a raging fireplace, a glass of wine, a good book. King of my castle. Screw the book; surely there was a good game on. A raging fire, a glass of wine, a good game. It was Saturday afternoon, Penn State versus Ohio State. Screw the wine. A raging fire, beer, the game.

I grabbed a bundle of my wood to unbundle it. It was wrapped in plastic. Impenetrable plastic. I tore at it, stretched it, bent back a fingernail. Couldn't get the damn plastic off. I succumbed to what I should have done in the first place. I grabbed a knife from the kitchen to jab at it and rip it open. Then I got a sharper knife and actually cut through the plastic. Liberated seasoned, kiln-dried firewood. I could hardly contain my excitement.

I stacked the firewood in the fireplace, after checking the flue (can't fool me twice). The bundle—thoughtfully, I thought—included some small sticks for kindling. I scattered them throughout the pile, took out a handy match and lit the sticks at a few strategic points. They burned. The flame and my spirits rose. The fire quietly gained strength and spread, creeping steadily along the lengths of the sticks. In a few moments, a flame caught at the corner of one of the larger logs. Then another. Then more. I was mesmerized. It was the dawn of man. Fire!

OK. Now to grab that beer, settle into my chair and enjoy the game, here in my four-bedroom, two-and-a-half bath, center-hall colonial country estate. This was living.

The fire was in full-blown cozy fireplace mode, the flames sprouting in intriguing shapes, a wisp of smoke flowing up the chimney in the right direction.

I actually rubbed my hands together as I headed for the refrigerator.

What the— Are you kidding me?

Laura! I yelled. Laura!

What? From somewhere deep in the bowels of the house.

Do we have any beer?

Look in the refrigerator.

I did look in the refrigerator. I'm looking in the refrigerator right now.

It was a conversation yelled between floors.

If we have any beer, it's in the refrigerator.

I don't see any.

Then we don't have any.

Why didn't you get beer?

It wasn't on the list.

What list?

The shopping list. She came into the kitchen, wiping her hands from, doubtlessly, the dust on some shelf somewhere.

Well, why the hell did it have to be on a list if you knew we didn't have any?

That's why we have a list. I buy what's on the list. When I run out of something, I put it on the list. Did you put beer on the list?

No. I just assumed that when we run out of something, you buy more.

Well, how would I know when we run out of something if it's not on the list?

I stared into the refrigerator, waiting for a bottle of beer to magically appear.

I'll pick some up.

Great! Thanks! Get it cold—so I can drink it now.

Wait. I'm not going to the store now. I'll pick it up when I go shopping.

When's that?

Tuesday.

I checked my pocket for my wallet, checked my fire— still raging—and called out matter-of-factly as I headed out the door,

Keep your eye on the fire. I'll be back in a few minutes.

There's a little liquor store next to Jimmy's.

I waited with my six-pack behind one other customer in the small, pretentiously named *shoppe*, as she chatted with the clerk. She'd been told that the red wines from West Virginia and North Carolina were just as good as the big-name California cabernets but half the price because of marketing. The clerk agreed and pointed to a pyramid display by the counter, saying that those wines were just as good as the ones in bottles.

Finally. Got my cold six-pack. Game on. Time to settle down with my fire. Pulled out my first beer, shoved the rest of the bottles into the fridge, and went in to grab some couch.

The fire was on its last legs, logs burned mostly to ashes, light flames flickering, feebly gasping to stay alive among the smoking cinders. It cast a sad pall over my Saturday afternoon, fire-fueled, me time.

I needed more wood.

I ripped open the second and last bundle and added the logs to the dwindling fire. In a few seconds, the fire came alive, picture perfect. I settled into my chair and twisted open my beer, sat back to watch the game.

No idea of the score or what was happening on the field, I was mesmerized by the fire, watching the flames lick at the logs, moving through the pile, darting here and there, consuming the wood. Consuming the wood. The wood was burning really well—and really fast. Maybe twenty minutes had passed, and the roaring fire had quieted to a small calm burning pile.

One of the teams was winning. I think the one in white.

The fire continued to peter out. Rather than a rush of flames in the fireplace, now a couple of individual logs lay burning, quiet and contentedly.

How's it going?

It's dying out.

Well, at least you got it lit. Was it fun?

Fun?

Yeah, did you have fun? Who's winning the game?

What game?

Aren't you watching the game?

Uh, yeah.

Who's winning?

Not sure.

Who's playing?

We need more firewood.

Really? Didn't you bring home those two big bundles?

Yeah, but they burned up pretty quickly.

Both of them?

Yeah. Took maybe an hour, hour and a half tops.

Wow.

Yeah, wow.

Is there such a thing as longer-burning wood?

Longer-burning wood? What's longer-burning wood?

I don't know. I just thought, you know, maybe you could ask someone.

One evening, later that week, Laura looked up from the paper.

There's an ad here for firewood. As a matter of fact, there are a couple of ads.

Firewood? Really? What do they say?

Firewood. Seasoned cut hardwood. Free delivery. There's a phone number.

OK. Call them.

I should call them?

Yeah. Call them.

I heard her on the phone in the kitchen.

Littleton. Yes. My husband said to make sure it's seasoned. Uh-huh. I'm not sure. A cord? You mean like one of those bundles? Maybe about twenty cords. How much would that be? How much?! How long would that last? How long?!

Yelling from the kitchen, He wants to talk to you.

Hello? Yeah. Well, how much is in a cord? How much?! I see. And how much per cord? Yeah. Is there such a thing as half a cord? Good. You deliver and pile it up? Yeah, right, stack it. Is it seasoned? OK. Gotta be seasoned. I want to use it now. OK. Great.

They're going to deliver it on Friday. We should have them stack it next to the path on the side of the house.

Are you sure about this? Seems like an awful lot of money for firewood. How many cords did you get?

II.

With a strong inclination toward denial and an unwillingness to simply accept at face value the flying mammalian observations of her obviously lunatic son, Laura was determined to investigate the bat matter herself.

The sun was finally setting on this white-hot sauna of a day. Cesar, the painter, and his helper, Guillermo, were done after a long day's work, ready to pack things up until tomorrow. They were drenched in sweat. Lean and muscular, they cleaned up in the driveway, packed up their gear, and then showered themselves with the garden hose. Despite the stifling heat, I'd never seen two guys work so hard for so long. It took them nearly an hour to clean themselves of the paint and sweat. A little self-conscious, I was glad they agreed to have a beer with me as the sun faded. We struggled through the language barrier to grouse about the heat, tapped our bottles together and enjoyed the refreshment. Good guys.

Laura stood nearby, staring up at the house from a chosen vantage point out on the front lawn, her eyes pinned to the roofline as she occasionally and absently tossed a tennis ball to the dog. The light grew dim; Cesar and Guillermo departed. The mosquitos descended in force, sending me slapping and swatting back into the house. Laura stood vigilant, scouring the skies for any sign of bats.

Come on in, already, I eventually called to her from an upstairs window. There are no bats.

Just a few more minutes. I keep thinking Jason must have seen something.

Come on, you're getting eaten alive out there. It's getting dark. You won't be able to see anything anyway.

Just a min— Oh my god!

What?

Bats! Bats are flying out of the house! Bats! Oh my god!

She came running into the house, hands clasped around her head, screaming for the dog to follow.

What? I said.

Bats. There are a million bats. They came flying out of the house. Like a cloud. Millions of them. Really. I mean hundreds, thousands. We have to do something! We have to do something!

Really? Bats?

Yes, really. We're living with bats. It's like it's their house, and we're living with them. All these years. Bats! We've got to get rid of them. We've got to do something.

What are we going to do?

I don't know. Call someone. We've got to get rid of these bats.

I guess we can call an exterminator.

Well, we better call someone!

After a sleepless night, I got in touch with the town wildlife-control guy. Turns out you can't exterminate bats. Technically, you're not supposed to kill bats. Apparently, bats are an important element in the ecosystem. Laura made it clear that she was a more important element in the ecosystem, and she was invoking her Darwinian privilege to oust the bats. She wanted no part of them.

In a feeble attempt to calm things, I tried to explain that bats were quite helpful and that many people put up bat houses on their property to attract them and keep the insect population under control.

Laura patiently explained exactly where I could shove my bat house.

Officer Bonaparte arrived in an army-green pickup truck with the town seal painted on the side. The town seal depicts an Indian shaking hands with what appears to be a real estate agent. There were a bunch of ominous empty cages in the back of the truck. The baby-faced Bonaparte worked his way out of the vehicle, a bit of a struggle since he was about five feet tall and five feet wide. He wore what I can only describe as a khaki Boy Scout uniform with short pants, complete with wide-brimmed hat and chin strap. He had a handgun holstered at his side, attached to a black leather belt that split him in two at the waist like a string tied around the equator of a balloon.

What's the problem? All business. Officious. The very model of a modern major general—or small-town civil servant.

Hello, Officer. Seems we have bats.

Yeah. Not unusual. They like houses like yours out here.

Well, we don't like them, said Laura. She folded her arms across her chest and shuddered. Please, we need to get rid of them. Do you, um, exterminate them?

Oh, we don't kill them. You can't kill them. Let's have a look.

OK, do you want to come upstairs? I asked, assuming he'd want to take a look at the bat residence in the attic.

No, I'll look around out here.

Officer Bonaparte wandered around the perimeter of the house, looking up occasionally but more interested in the ground.

Yep. You've got bats, he said. Lookit here.

He pointed down at the driveway just in front of the garage doors. The ground was scattered with tiny black curly wormlike things. Hundreds, thousands of them, all there in front of the garage doors.

What's that? I asked.

Bat droppings.

What?

Bat droppings. You know, bat droppings. Waste. From the bats.

Batshit!

Officer Bonaparte flinched a little.

Looks like you've got a sizeable population living in the attic.

Rent free, I said, trying to lighten things up.

Well, what do you do? When can you get rid of them? What do you do, poison them or something?

Oh no. It's illegal to poison them. We don't kill bats.

What do you mean, it's illegal? What do we do? We can't live here with bats. I could see Laura was way beyond uncomfortable.

You have to perform a proper live exclusion.

A what?

A proper live exclusion.

What would be an improper live exclusion, I wondered.

I don't know what you mean, I said. What do we do? We can't continue living here with these bats. How do we do one of these exclusions? What the hell is a live exclusion?

I can give you the name of the regional wildlife-control warden. He's licensed by the state, and he can help you.

That's it?

That's it for me. Don't worry; they won't hurt you or anything. They pretty much just sleep during the day, then go out to feed at night. They shouldn't bother you.

I don't care! We're not running a bat bed-and-breakfast here, said Laura. We've got to get rid of them. She turned to me, Please, we have got to get rid of them!

Here. Officer Bonaparte handed me a business card. Walsh J. Brickhauser Jr., Regional Wildlife Control Officer. Give him a call.

Thanks.

Yep. Tipped his hat.

He waddled back to his truck and departed.

Ah, Old Brickhauser. We knew him well.

Well, now what?

Now we call Brickhauser, I guess. I sang, Didi didi didi didi, didi didi didi didi, Batman!

She didn't sing along.

You call him. I'm going to take a shower. I'm going crazy from this heat, and I'm feeling so dirty from these bats.

You can't shower. Cesar is painting up in the bedroom.

Oh god, kill me now.

She clasped her hands to her temples. I've got to get some ice for my head.

Brickhauser was a big strapping guy, an aging woodsman. His receding, graying blond hair was pulled back into a ponytail and matched a bushy drooping Fu Manchu mustache. He wore scruffy, shapeless, frayed khakis, work boots and a worn, faded denim shirt with the sleeves rolled up his thick forearms, revealing a tattoo of a mermaid swinging on an anchor on one arm and a big-eyed owl on the other. He got out of an old red, dusty pickup truck, paused for a moment to size up the situation, then walked over and extended a big beefy hand. Huge hand.

How ya doin'?

We knew him as the raccoon guy.

A couple of years earlier, the raccoon incident brought our first encounter with Officer Bonaparte and, as it turned out, Brickhauser.

A huge old tulip tree stands at the crest of a hill that overlooks our property. Our house sits right in its path should it fall, and I was always worried it would fall. Though ours is the house that's threatened, technically the tree is on our neighbor's property. The tree's not in great shape. Every time there's a stiff wind or a bit of a breeze or if someone sneezes, some rotted branches fall from above and land on our driveway. That tree scares the hell out of me. With every storm warning I have visions of it crashing down on our house. I've talked to the neighbors about having it taken down, always offering to pay half the cost. They agree, then we have a tree guy come out to take a look and give us an estimate. It's usually a big old guy smelling of cigar smoke, who stands in our driveway and stares up into the spreading branches.

Yeah, I can see why you'd want to take her down.

Yeah, well, what would it cost?

Well, we'd have to get a truck back in here, then drop it across the driveway onto the lawn. Can't guarantee you won't have some damage. As a matter of fact, I can pretty much guarantee you will have damage. That there's a big mother.

Yeah, well what would it cost?

Well, it's a pretty big job. Have to send my climbers up there. Take a couple few days. Would you want the wood?

No. I want the whole thing down and out of here. What would it cost?

Those power lines are in the way. Same with that cable wire. Boy, it'd be a bear dropping it down that hill. Gonna be a mess.

Yeah, well, what would it cost?

Let me give it some thought, and I'll get back to you.

When? When can you get back to me with an estimate?

What's today, Tuesday? Thursday, Friday. I'll give you a call. Let me take down your information.

He could have been writing down his daily horoscope, for all it was worth. Never heard from him again.

We had three or four other guys come out. Similar experiences. Every now and again there'd be a big storm. I'd worry about the tree and have someone come out and take a look. Same result. One time a guy pulled up in his truck, got out and looked at the tree, shook his head, got back in his truck and just left.

The tree still stands.

About a third of the way up the trunk there are a couple of big old hollowed-out holes. One afternoon, I was standing at my office window, which looks out at the tree, and I saw a raccoon nestled into the opening of one of the holes, lounging there like Alice's Cheshire cat. I could swear he was smoking a pipe. Then I noticed the other raccoons, moving in and out of the holes; the whole family had made themselves at home in the tulip tree. It freaked me out. Everyone knows that raccoons are mean mothers that carry rabies. I worried about the dog, the kids, Laura. Most of all, I worried about me. The things gave me the creeps. I wanted them off our property and out of our tree.

Laura! Laura!

What?

We've got raccoons!

What?

We've got raccoons! There's a whole damn family of raccoons living in the tulip tree.

What do you mean living in the tulip tree? Where?

There. Up there, I pointed. Look up there. There's a whole family of them. Sleazy little mothers.

Ewwwww. God, look at them. They're creepy.

Don't they say you shouldn't see raccoons in the daytime? Doesn't that mean they have rabies or something?

I don't know. I don't know anything about raccoons. They don't attract bears, do they?

Who cares about bears. We've got real raccoons.

What should we do? Who can we ask?

Who can we ask? How about the Town Department of Raccoons in Trees?

I don't know. I'll call Ellen Majewski.

The Majewskis were our neighbors down the lane. They were the elders of our little woodsy community and had been living there long before we arrived. They pretty much served as our authorities on everything Littleton.

Laura went to call. The raccoons made themselves at home, puttering and prowling about the tree, two lying in the hole opening, one stretched out on a branch. I'm not sure, but I think I saw the blue light of a TV inside the tree. Through my binoculars, I could see them looking back at me.

OK. Ellen says to call Officer Bonaparte at the town hall. He's the animal control warden.

That's it. We'll bring in the law. Call the guy.

And that's when we first met Officer Bonaparte—when he came out to look at our raccoons.

They don't look rabid or nothing, said Bonaparte, staring up at the tree.

Well, what should we do?

Not much you can do. It's pretty much their home as much as it is yours.

Oh yeah? I don't see them chipping in for the mortgage.

Well, there's not really much you can do about them.

The man had no sense of humor whatsoever.

Laura was having a hard time with this. Isn't there something you can do? How do we get rid of them? They're really creepy. Aren't they dangerous? Do you trap them or something?

Well, I can't kill them unless they're rabid. It's illegal to kill them if they're healthy.

Can't we just shoot them?

No, sir. You can't fire a weapon on land this close to a residence.

I didn't really mean to shoot them, I was just saying.

Well, you cannot discharge a firearm in this area. Period.

Bonaparte didn't mess around. Anything else I can do for you?

Anything *else*? I said. He didn't get it.

Well, they're healthy. Shouldn't be a problem. Make sure you secure your garbage. Keep it inside your garage with the garage doors closed. If they can, they'll get in there and make a pretty big mess. Also, stay away from them. They can be a little mean.

That was the first time he gave us Walsh J. Brickhauser Jr.'s card.

Brickhauser sounded almost bored on the phone. Deep, gravelly voice.

Yeah, sure. I can come out there and take a look.

What time can you be here?

Tuesday.

Tuesday?

Yeah, I can get out there Tuesday morning.

Well, if you need anything, my wife can pick it up at the store.

Pardon?

Never mind. Can't you get here before Tuesday? What are we supposed to do until Tuesday?

Whatever you want. The raccoons won't bother you. Did Bonaparte say they were rabid?

No, he said they looked healthy. They watch what they eat and work out three or four times a week.

Huh?

Bonaparte said they were healthy.

No worries, then. Just keep your distance, and keep your trash locked up.

Do you need directions?

No, I know where you are. End of that long lane, right?

Yes.

I got it.

Laura was waiting to hear.

Tuesday. He'll be here Tuesday morning.

Tuesday? What are we supposed to do until Tuesday?

Make a shopping list?

What are you talking about?

Never mind. He says just to stay away from them and make sure the trash is locked up. There's only one thing that worries me.

Worries you? What's that?

He knows where we are. He knows our house. You think he's been here before?

For what?

That's what worries me.

It was probably a mistake to take the call during a client dinner, but, you know, it was Laura, and she was home alone and you never know. I answered and excused myself.

There's a raccoon in the garage! More a scream than a statement. There's a raccoon in the garage! A raccoon! There's an effing raccoon in the garage!

Who is this?

It's not funny. Don't joke around. There's a raccoon in the garage. Do something.

Do something? What am I going to do? I'm in Atlanta. I'm at dinner.

I don't care where you are. You'd better do something. I want that thing out of the garage.

How did it get in the garage?

It made a left turn after the flowerbed! How did it get in? I forgot to close the garage doors. I went to take out the trash, and the thing was sitting there on top of the trashcan, staring at me.

What did you do?

What did I do? I dropped the trash and came back in the house. I'm not going out there again. You've got to do something! You've got to get rid of it.

Well, I can't do anything from here.

Well, you'd better do something.

OK, put it on the phone.

This is no time for your jokes. I'm not kidding. I want that thing out of here.

OK, OK. Let me think. Call DeNino. Maybe he can help.

Peter DeNino is our neighbor, a construction contractor. He does stuff.

OK. Good idea. I'll call you back.

I returned to the table and apologized.

Sorry, minor emergency at home.

Everything OK?

Yeah. Raccoons.

Did you say raccoons?

Yeah. We've got some raccoons visiting.

Is that a euphemism for in-laws?

Unfortunately, no.

Real raccoons? Hey, they can be nasty.

Yeah, said the other guy, just like in-laws.

A little later, the phone again.

Hello?

It's gone.

What happened?

Peter came over and got rid of it.

What did he do?

I don't know. I called him and told him about the raccoon, and he drove around and went into the garage. A few minutes later he knocked on the door and said it was gone. He told me he closed the garage doors and that it was gone. I'm still not going out there, though.

All right. Well, I'll be home tomorrow.

What a relief.

I didn't know if she was talking about me coming home, talking about me with sarcasm, or referring to the dispatching of the raccoon. I didn't ask.

Well, I'm not going out there again until the raccoon guy comes on Tuesday. You can go out there this weekend. I'm not going anywhere near that garage or near that tree. I can't believe we have raccoons.

Yeah, Brickhauser said as he shielded his eyes and looked up into the tree. A whole family of 'em. Not rabid, though. They're fine.

Fine? Yeah, they're fine, said Laura. We're not fine. We have raccoons. What do we do about them?

Not much you can do.

Um, I could really use a better answer than that. We've got to get rid of them somehow.

Well, you're allowed to capture and remove them, but you can't kill them. Not if they're healthy.

I think I heard one of them cough.

Huh?

OK, so how do we capture and remove them? Traps?

Well, I'm not sure that'd work out real well. You might get one or two, but we won't get all of them.

Brickhauser hadn't taken his eyes off the tree, watching the raccoons move around inside the hole and along the branches. He stood quietly for a while, looking up at the tree. After a few moments, he looked down and went up to investigate the ground around the tree trunk, then the tree trunk itself, running his hand over it.

Lots of tracks, he said. They're coming down at night, going out looking for food.

He looked around a little more.

Here's what I think, he said. I think these guys are just in their migratory path. This is just a stopping station for them. I'll bet they're out of here in a couple of days.

Yeah, well, their reservation is up, and checkout time is now.

Pardon?

Nothing. So what do we do?

I'd wait.

Wait for what?

Like I said, I think they're just stopping here. I bet they're gone in a couple of days. How long they been here?

I noticed them last week.

Yeah, they'll be gone in another day or two.

That's it?

Yeah. Give me a call at the end of the week if they're not gone—or if you see any of them kind of stumbling around in the daytime.

You think they're drinking?

Huh?

That's it?

That's it. You'll be OK. Keep the trash locked up.

I just had to ask before he left.

Hey, how did you know where we were?

What do you mean?

When we talked on the phone, you said you knew the place. Were you here before?

Yeah. Previous owners, I guess. Stephens, Stevenson, something like that.

Stephenson.

Yeah. One time they had a big dead woodchuck. Kept it under a bucket in the back till I got here. Nothing to do about it really; just hauled it away.

What is it with all this? Raccoons, woodchucks?

Well, it's the woods, you know. They were here first.

Great. We're living in *Wild Kingdom*.

III.

That was then. This time Walsh J. Brickhauser Jr. pulled up in his old red pickup with a ladder loaded in the bed, parked next to the painter's van, got out and sauntered across the driveway through the rolling waves of heat like a gunman in an old Western.

Whatcha got? he said.

Bats.

Bats, huh. He looked over the house at the trees and woods beyond. Yeah. You're in the right place for 'em. They must love it here.

How do we get rid of them? Laura nearly pleaded. Do we have to fog the house or something? What?

You folks had the raccoons that time. In the tree. Right?

Yeah, that was us.

He looked up at the tulip tree, still standing, threatening.

OK, now. Bats. He turned his attention to the problem at hand, wandered over to the house, avoiding the paint supplies scattered over the driveway, and began walking the perimeter—much like Officer Bonaparte.

Yeah, droppings all over, he said, studying the ground. Sizeable population too. Probably been here for years. Once they find a place they like, they keep coming back year after year. Bet they like it here.

We're so proud, I said.

Laura looked like she was about to cry. She just wanted something done.

How do we get rid of them? she asked again.

He ignored the question and went over and pulled the ladder from the back of the pickup. He hoisted it on his shoulder, hauled it over to the house, set it down and pulled on some ropes that somehow extended the ladder all the way to the roof. He tested that it was steady, then climbed to the roofline. I watched him climb, shielding my eyes from the sun. Laura stood with her arms stiff at her sides, awaiting the worst.

Yeah, I can hear 'em, he yelled down.

Laura shuddered.

He climbed down, pulled down the ladder and carried it back to the truck, then came over to give us his professional assessment. He moved deliberately, in no particular hurry.

Well, you got bats all right.

We get it, I said. Now how do we kill them?

Oh, we don't kill them. You can't kill them. Besides, you don't want to kill them.

Yes. Yes, I do.

No, you can't kill them.

All right, so, please already, pleaded Laura, what do we do?

We exclude them.

Exclude them? What, like we don't let them into the country club? I asked only half facetiously.

Yeah, something like that.

What does that mean exactly?

Well, see, the bats go out at night looking for food. They feed on insects. They eat a ton of insects. Lots of people like to keep them around because they eat all the insects.

Well, let's say we're not interested in providing an all-you-can-eat bat buffet. We just want to get rid of them. What do we do?

Well, when they go out to feed, when it's near morning, they want to return to, in your case, the attic. That's their home.

Yeah?

So what we have to do is, we have to make it so they can't get back to their home. We got to seal it off.

Yeah?

Yeah. We let 'em out, but we don't let them back in.

So? Laura looked at Brickhauser, waiting for more information.

So what we do is we seal up the entire house, then we put up bat doors.

Bat doors?

Yeah. First, we've got to seal up any spaces around the perimeter of the attic where they can get in. Any cracks that can let them inside, we got to seal them up good. Close down all the windows. Everything sealed up tight, no cracks.

Seal the windows?! In this heat?! With the paint fumes?! Are you kidding me?

Nope, that's what you have to do. Seal up the house completely, nice and tight. When those bats come back in the morning, they'll try to get in any way they can, and they can get through even the smallest crack.

My god.

What's this about bat doors?

Yeah. See they fly in primarily through the air vents in the roof. See those vents up there? On the side of the house, up where the attic is?

Yeah. I'd never noticed them before.

They're ventilation for the attic, let the heat out, air out, keeps the house from retaining moisture or stagnating. Ventilates the attic. The bats generally go in through those vents. There are several of them, if you look around the top of the house.

OK.

So, the bats use the vents to get back into the attic in the morning. What we do is we hang mesh down over the vents, extend it down below the vents themselves. See, the bats can get out by going down and out, but they can't get back under the mesh and go up to get back in. Once we seal the place up and hang our bat doors, the bats will go out to feed at night, but they won't be able to get back in in the morning. After a while, they'll get tired of trying to get in and take off for somewhere else. Bats gone.

OK, I brightened. Sounds like a plan.

You sure this works? Laura seemed skeptical.

Oh, sure. We do it all the time.

We? I wondered aloud.

Yeah. My guys will seal up the place and hang the bat doors.

My guys? I thought. Here it comes.

If we do this, how much is it going to cost?

81

Laura didn't let him answer but turned to me.

If? What do you mean, if? IF we don't get rid of the bats, THEN I'm leaving. She turned to Brickhauser.

When can you do this?

So Brickhauser looked up at the house and stroked his mustache, calculations running through his head. Well, I can get the guys here tomorrow. Big population—cost about a milliondyhundred dollars.

Laura responds at precisely the same time I do:

Fine.

How much?!

Despite the suffering in the summertime heat, the real agony in our house comes in winter.

First off, the long lane leading to our house presents a challenge whenever it snows. The ride up that lane is seriously being considered as a Winter Olympics event. The narrow roadway winds through the woods, with a significant falloff on either side. At one point, there's an abrupt bend in the road that turns up a steep hill, bordered by a sharp incline that tumbles down into the woods. You get points for speed, style and arriving at the top without killing yourself.

Our first winter in the house, before I started working at home, I set off for the office after a fairly minor snowfall, carefully navigating the slick roadway. I approached the hill, considering whether it would be better to stop and proceed slowly, or get a running start and let momentum carry me up. I hit the gas pedal and was cheering myself on until, about half way up, my forward progress stalled, wheels spinning in place. I hit the brake and felt myself sliding back down the hill. I panicked. If the car slid straight back, I'd slide right off the hill into the woods. I talked to the car—yelled at the car—*Stop. Stop.* Come on, stop. I turned in my seat, one hand on the wheel, staring wide-eyed through the rear window, trying to somehow influence my fate. I had no control. I made many promises.

Somehow, the car came to a stop without tumbling off the side of the road. I sat rigid in my driver's seat, staring straight ahead, hands frozen to the steering wheel, heart thumping in my chest, trying to regain my composure. OK. I was in one piece. Whew. Close call. That was a little scary.

I paused to thank the deity for sparing me, grateful that I would experience many more winters to come, and bask in the years ahead with my family, affording plenty of time to pay off the kids' inevitable student loans. Then I thought, I can make it if I hit the hill a little faster, and that'll propel me up and over the crest at the top. I'll be home free.

I backed up a little ways down the lane, gripped the wheel, paused to gather my wits, gritted my teeth, put it in gear and hit the gas. Up, up, aha! Up, up and... NOOOOOOO! The wheels went into a spin. I cursed and gunned it. The tires screamed back. I turned the wheel right and left, trying to get a grip on the road. Nothing. Then gravity. The backslide started. No control. Down, down. Oh crap! I squeezed my eyes shut, waiting for the worst. Again, I somehow came to a stop at the bottom of the hill, this time even closer to the side ditch.

I opened my door to have a look, and there wasn't enough room to get out of the car without falling down the hill. This wasn't going to work. I wasn't going to work. We were trapped in the woods, prisoners of the snow and our bucolic country lane. If only I had a snowblower.

I was sitting in the car, taking stock of the situation. Then I heard it before I saw it. Through the woods beyond the hill was a large pickup truck with a plow on the front, clearing the snow from the lane up ahead. He stopped short of our section of the lane, maneuvered the truck around and headed back in the opposite direction. I somehow managed to extricate myself from the car through the passenger side door and, slipping and sliding, climbed the hill, running and waving to get the guy's attention.

Hey! Hey! I yelled, waving my arms like I was signaling to a search-and-rescue plane. He surely couldn't hear me over the scraping of the plow, shut inside his truck's cab, so I had to run all the way up to him, nearly putting myself in the plow's path to get his attention.

Hey, there. What's up? He lowered the window.

I couldn't say anything. I was trying to catch my breath.

You OK?

I bobbed my head to say yes but still couldn't talk.

You sure you're OK?

I nodded up and down again, steadying myself against the truck. Finally, I found my voice.

Hi.

Hi.

You plow? My keen powers of observation.

Yeah, that's what I'm doing.

Right. I still struggled a little to catch my breath.

Well, what's the deal? Can you plow down there, I pointed, further down the lane?

You the new folks in number 20?

Yeah. Moved in over the summer. Breath, word, breath, word.

Hi, I'm Mitch.

Steve.

Yeah, I can plow if you want.

Great. What's the deal?

The way it works is I plow the common area of the road, then divvy up the bill for all the houses on the lane here. That's only for the common part of the road, though.

I vaguely remembered this from when we bought the house. Something about everyone chipping in for the snowplow—minimum cost, couple of times a year, nothing to worry about. I didn't pay much attention at the time.

If you want, I can plow your part of the road, but you have to pay for that yourself.

Well, how much would that be?

Well, I think your portion of the common charge is about sixteen dollars. We don't charge the old folks at number 24. Then, to go down and do your part of the road would be another forty. If you want, I can do your whole driveway too for another fifteen.

So, for all that, each snowfall would cost me seventy-one bucks?

Yeah, I guess that's right.

But the snow would be all cleared?

Yeah, sure.

Every time it snowed?

Yeah, seventy-one each time. Well, whenever it snows more than four inches, anyway.

Four inches?

Yeah, less than that and it's not really worth it.

OK, then, let's add our house to the list.

Okeydoke. He reached over to grab something in the truck and handed me his card: Mitch Slater, Plowing, with his number.

You want me to just come automatically, or do you want to decide each time?

Just come automatically. If it snows, I need to get the road and driveway cleared.

You got it. Just call if you need anything.

Thanks.

Yup. After I finish up here, I'll be down to your place.

Great. Just got to get my car out of the way.

So that's how Mitch the Plow Guy became an integral part of our lives—or as I referred to him, Mitch the Ineffectual Snowplow Guy.

You'd think the deal with Mitch would have solved the snow problems, but no, it was just the beginning.

The snow would fall. We couldn't get out of the driveway. We'd wait for Mitch. We'd occupy ourselves around the house, trapped by the snow, looking out through the windows, peering up the lane for a sign of the plow. Waiting, waiting, for Mitch to set us free.

Laura would call. He'd be right over, he'd say. Within the hour.

And we'd wait some more.

I'm on my way, he'd say at the next call. Fifteen minutes.

And we'd wait some more.

Laura is always very nice to Mitch on the phone, very patient, very understanding. Without him, we'd never get out. Without the snowplow, we're up the proverbial creek without a shovel.

We knew that beyond the lane, in the rest of the town, things were normal. People were shopping, children were playing, lives were being lived. Here in the tundra, life was at a standstill. Waiting, waiting, for the plow guy. Without Mitch, we couldn't get fuel oil. The trash couldn't be picked up. No one could go in or out without some version of a Hummer.

Finally, sometimes late at night, we'd hear the truck coming down the lane, scraping the snow in its path, plowing the lane, pushing the snow from the driveway into big piles that blocked the garage. But, hey, we were just glad he showed up at all.

He's here! He's here! We'd call out. The plow's here! There was rejoicing throughout the land. Free at last, free at last!

Unfortunately, only then did the work begin.

Mitch plowed the snow out of the way, all right, but nearly always left behind a thick sheet of ice. Mitch plowed the snow, but he didn't drop sand or salt to effectively clear the road. It was too expensive, he said. He'd have to charge much more, and, besides, his truck really wasn't equipped to lay sand and salt behind him. This was a topic of conversation among the neighbors from time to time, but no one else was trapped at the bottom of the hill with each snowstorm, so it really wasn't a high priority for them, especially at the additional cost. No, they'd stay with Mitch and plow through, so to speak.

So Laura and I became the road crew. All winter we stocked heavy bags of road salt in the garage. Once Mitch had finished his plowing, we'd don our road crew duds—heavy jeans, wool socks, work gloves, bulky down jackets over sweaters over sweatshirts over flannel shirts over T-shirts, boots with ice-gripping metal spikes attached (Laura) or, in my case, sneakers to keep from slipping. We'd pile bags of salt, shovels and buckets into the back of Laura's SUV and head up to the foot of the hill. There we'd unload, fill our buckets, and begin spreading the salt by hand, throwing it about like chicken feed, spreading the salt over the roadbed. More than once we fell on our asses. Our hands grew numb as it became difficult to handle the last of the salt with our gloves on. Our backs hurt, our knees ached. How we avoided broken bones I'll never know. I fumed the whole time, every time. Laura, oddly, approached the whole task with a perverse joy. She loved being out in the invigorating cold, doing something useful. As soon as Mitch was finished, she was up and out in the garage, loading up the car with salt, road crew at the ready. She was full of cheer. I could kill her.

So we'd salt the hill, freeing ourselves to escape the house and get up the lane. In town, we'd see that the rest of the world was carrying on quite normally. It never ceased to confound me that the entire town was completely unaffected by the snow, while we sat isolated, trapped in an icebound fortress of solitude, our only hope being that Mitch had a boat payment due.

Even so, the plowing and the salting still isn't my biggest winter problem. My biggest problem is that, inexplicably, somewhere along the line, Laura is apparently descended from Eskimos—an Eskimo from Queens, New York. She loves the cold. And this fondness for everything frosty is foisted upon the whole household.

In the winter, it is always cold in our house. There's no other way to put it. It is always cold—teeth-chattering, shoulder-shivering cold. Throughout the house. It's below freezing outside; the news stories are all about winter snowstorms and bitter temperatures, record lows, cold fronts stuck in place, no thaw in sight. In our house, Laura has the windows open. I'm walking around the house, arms clasped around my body, complaining, Why is it so cold in here? Jeez, it's colder in our house than it is outside.

Our conversations are always the same.

Well, look at you. Look what you're wearing. All you've got on is a sweatshirt. Look at me, I'm wearing layers. I've got a shirt, another shirt, a sweater and a vest.

Not to mention, you're curled up under a blanket.

Yes. That's how you're supposed to dress in the winter.

Why? Why can't we be comfortable in our own home? We have the modern miracle of a heating system. Since the dawn of man, our species has been building structures and dwellings to protect us from the elements. We have a nice house, with a heater; why does it have to be so cold?

It's healthy. Fresh air.

Fresh air?! Icicles are forming under my nostrils.

Come on. It's good. It's healthy. You should dress properly.

Why should I have to dress in eighty-two layers just to walk around my own house? It's insane.

Stop being so dramatic.

But that's not the worst part. The worst part is at night. It's the dead of winter, and we're not allowed to have the heat on in the bedroom. She's got the windows wide open.

As you ascend the stairs to our bedroom, smoke comes out of your mouth. Walking into our bedroom at night is like walking into a meat locker. If I get up in the middle of the night, I step on the floor, and my feet hurt from the cold. I keep a bottle of water on my nightstand, and there's ice floating in it.

It's lunacy, I tell her. We have a thermostat. You set it on a comfortable temperature, and let it be.

Well, what temperature do you want?

Oh, I don't know, say seventy. Something normal.

Seventy?! Are you kidding? We'll be sweating like pigs! Seventy.

That's a normal temperature. OK. Sixty-eight. Sixty-five. Something, anything in the sixties would be good.

Come on, we don't need the heat. Sixties?

Well, what do you think a normal temperature should be?

Well, not the sixties.

What then?

Lower, cooler.

Look, I say, if it's fifty degrees outside, you put on a jacket to go out, right? Now why should that be the temperature in our bedroom?

That's my point. You're not dressed properly. You need to dress in layers.

What is this, boot camp? Boy Scout training? Arctic survival drills for the Navy SEALS?

Stop being so dramatic. If you want the heat on, put the heat on. I don't care.

OK. I'm putting the heat on.

Fine.

And I'm closing the windows.

No. That's where I draw the line. We're not closing the windows. We need some fresh air in here. The windows stay open.

It was in trying to come to grips with the cold, to accommodate the winter, that I finally acquiesced one year and agreed that, as a family, we'd take up skiing.

Now standing in line for coffee drives me crazy and starts me to grinding my teeth. My knees wobble, and I get dizzy if I climb so much as a four-foot step ladder to change a light bulb, and I tend to hibernate when the temperature drops below fifty degrees. Oh, skiing is the thing for me!

Bubbling, Laura thought it was a wonderful idea, a terrific family activity we could all do together. She was already planning family vacations to Colorado. The kids talked about going away with their friends on ski trips. My business partner was an avid skier and for years had been urging me to take it up and bring the family up to his condo in Vermont.

The skiing thing had been percolating for years. It finally got to me. One February day, half joke half surrender, I showed up at the office wearing ski pants. My partner took this as a sign, dropped what he was doing, and we drove over to his favorite ski shop where he walked me through a full outfitting. He relished it. Frankly, I think he just liked being an expert in something I knew nothing about, but he was in his element. Which skis would be good for me and why, what to stay away from, and the boots, the boots! How important were the boots! Poles and gloves and a jacket and socks and these warmer things for your hands and feet and goggles and a hat. At checkout, it cost eleventymillion dollars.

We went back to the office, and he skipped out, telling me not to leave before he got back. An hour later, he showed up with a bunch of skis and poles and boots. His kids' old stuff from various stages in their ski careers. Most of it almost brand new, he said. Some of this stuff would work for my kids. On the drive home that night, my car looked like the ski section of eBay had exploded in the back seat.

Laura was delighted. It's going to be great, she said, overflowing with enthusiasm. Out in the crisp air, skiing down the hills, all of us together. We can get hot chocolate after. I read about this place up near Kent, Mohawk Mountain, she said. Generations of Connecticut kids have learned to ski there, she was quoting from the online brochure. It's small, perfect for us. We can go on Saturday.

I sniffed. I think I feel a cold coming on.

You know, she said, even with all the stuff Tim gave you, we still need plenty. There aren't boots to fit everyone and not enough poles, and we still need skis.

So we all got in the car and drove over to Skis-R-Us. As we all walked in together, I'm certain I saw the salesman leap into the air, clapping. Eleventymillion times four.

We drove up to Mohawk on Saturday, parked and struggled across a muddy, icy parking lot, trudging along, toting our new equipment like pack mules, making our way up to the lodge.

Look, Laura said, pointing to a line of people queued up under a big sign. We could've rented everything.

We split up to our respective locker rooms to change into our gear. The boys seemed to pick things up pretty quickly, but, despite several demonstrations back at the ski store, I couldn't get the hang of putting on my boots and getting them set in my skis. This was in spite of the uninterested, even condescending assistance of the pimply faced teenage locker room attendant who was there to help so that the bindings would *cut loose in a fall and you won't break your leg.*

When we all met again outside the locker rooms, I caught the aroma of grilled food wafting from a vast cafeteria.

Hey, the burgers look good, I ventured.

We came here to ski, not to eat. Let's go. Our lesson starts in ten minutes.

Laura had asked someone and arranged to enroll us in a New Skiers Group Lesson. Adults welcome.

Jason and Matt, expressing no tolerance for taking lessons with, in their words, a bunch of kindergartners, disappeared immediately, saying, We'll catch up with you later.

Laura and I somehow hobbled over to a designated area, where we became part of a group of fewer than a dozen earnest novices yearning to speed down mountains on slivers of fiberglass. It was a mixed group, kids and a few adults, but Laura and I were clearly the tribal elders.

Laura was her usual social self, assuming hostess duties until the instructors arrived—making introductions and talking about how exciting it all was, and wasn't it a great day, and it was going to be such fun.

I was calculating: OK, the lesson is an hour, then we hang out for another hour, then I can reasonably start talking about heading home.

Our instructors arrived. Kenny and Kendra. The really, really blond Kenny and Kendra. An actual shine radiated from their faces, or maybe it was their teeth. Kenny wore a fierce black outfit with neon-yellow lightening-stripe accents. Kendra wore a pink and powder-blue outfit that defined cute. They didn't wear hats. I wished I could take off my ridiculous green-and-white-striped wool hat with the little pompom on top; my ears itched. But I couldn't do anything with the damn gloves on. Kenny and Kendra smiled. They talked about what fun we were going to have.

They said we'd be heading up the lift and skiing down the mountain in no time.

First things first, they said. We needed to learn how to walk. They said this cheerfully. They said everything cheerfully. They showed us how to walk using a crisscross pattern with their skis, then demonstrated how to use the edge of the skis to dig into the snow and make our way up the slightest of inclines. They went first and everyone followed, each with his or her own little version of the ski walk. Some, the kids mostly, had immediate success. Others, of course, had a more difficult time, sliding back down the little incline, struggling to move forward. One guy, Marty, a little younger than me, seemed to pick up everything quickly and appointed himself group coach. As if it wasn't enough that he was a cocksure loudmouth, he wore a long, pointed, red knitted ski cap with a white pompom on the end that hung down to his shoulder. YALE was knitted into the front of his cap. He kept giving instructions on how to do what we were doing. If Marty was so damn good at it, what was he doing here in our beginners' group? What, he flunked his first time through and now was taking it pass-fail? A little stronger, Marty would say. Stick your leg right in there; get that ski stuck in the snow. Stick it right in there.

Hey, Marty, stick it right—

Despite my struggles and those of a few of my classmates, Kenny and Kendra kept saying, That's it. That's it. You got it. There you go.

Didn't matter if we were moving forward or not. According to Kenny and Kendra, we were doing great.

It didn't take but a few minutes before I realized that Kenny's eyes and attention had locked onto the teenage Kimmy. It was pretty clear. If your name wasn't Kimmy, Kenny didn't even see you. Kenny fawned. Kimmy giggled. Kendra's attention was focused on two twins (no, three twins?), maybe seven or eight years old. The rest of us basically had to fend for ourselves.

We'd been at it for maybe ten minutes, sliding down the little incline, then waddling back up, when I slipped and fell. Crap. I couldn't get up. I reached for Laura, who was no help at all. No way she was letting go of her poles to reach out to me. Kenny was chatting it up with Kimmy. Kendra was holding hands with and encouraging one of the young angel twins.

Every time I tried to get my skis under me to stand up, they slid out from under, and I fell back down. I felt like an overturned turtle.

What was I doing here?

After more than several attempts to rise, I just lay back in the snow and stayed there. Screw it. I watched cottony clouds float across the clear blue sky. I imagined the blissfulness of freezing to death right there in the Connecticut hillside while eight-year-olds whizzed by. Gathering my wits, I gained clarity. I'll just lie here, I thought, until everyone gets tired, then we can all go home.

Kenny, of all people, finally came over and helped me up.

There you go, he beamed, pulling me to my feet, er, skis, all the while looking straight at Kimmy, showing himself to be the patient, tolerant hero of the snowily challenged.

I said thanks, but he was already gone, laughing it up with young Kim.

Just keep practicing, said Kendra. Ski down, then walk your way back up. You'll get the hang of it.

We kept at it. There was nothing else to do. There were a few falls, but we managed to help each other out a little. After what seemed like a week of sliding down this little incline and then walking back up, I looked around. Kenny and Kendra were nowhere to be found. Kimmy was gone too. What was there to do? Slide down, walk up. Slide down, walk up.

After a while, Kendra returned, smiling like she was in a toothpaste commercial.

OK, guys, she beamed, now you're ready for the Dolly Parton! Come on!

She led the way to a small, snow-covered bump, mound, hill that kind of sat off to the side in an out-of-the-way corner.

There you go—your first mountain! She pointed emphatically with an outstretched arm, inviting us to take in the looming challenge.

Let's go, she cheered us on, effortlessly making her way to the top of the small hill. We lumbered behind, concentrating on our ski walk. There was barely enough space at the top to gather, and everyone jockeyed to stay away from the incline lest they lose control and go sliding down the Dolly Parton.

Everyone here? Kendra looked around. You OK, guys? She looked to the twins, who gave her enthusiastic dual thumbs-up.

OK, now watch, she said, with a flip of her pole, and she glided easily to the bottom of the short hill and spun around on her skis to face us.

That's all there is to it. I had to shield my eyes from her smile. Now you guys, one at a time.

Marty said he'd go first.

If there truly is a god, I prayed, Marty will fall flat on his ass.

There is no god.

Piece of cake, Marty beamed from the bottom of the hill—literally, thirty feet away. Nothing to it.

See, said Kendra, just like Marty. You can all do it!

I can't be entirely sure, but I thought I saw Marty bow. I had a vision that, someday, having mastered the slopes, I'd go flying right by Marty and skewer him with a ski pole.

Haltingly, one at a time, we gave ourselves a slight push with our ski poles and slid down the little hill. We slid down the hill OK. What we couldn't do was stop. While some of us were going so slow it didn't matter, a couple of us, including me, slid right past Kendra. Several yards beyond. Even on this little hill and tiny little trip, I was disconcerted at the lack of control and let out a cartoonish *Whoooaaaa*, to the great amusement of the gallery.

OK, explained Kendra, deliberately looking directly at me. There are two ways to stop. You can pull your skis sideways and dig into the snow, or, if you're not ready for that, you can kind of point the front of your skis together in a *V* to slow down, but be careful not to let them cross.

Now that's where Kendra was way wrong. There are lots of other ways to stop, and in the hour that followed, I tried a bunch of them:

You can just glide along until the snow-covered ground suddenly ends, where you come to a shockingly abrupt halt and tumble face forward into the icy mud.

You can grab onto some stranger's jacket as you slide by and hang on for dear life, toppling the both of you to the ground, and wait for some kindly kid to come help you up.

You can squat down low on your skis, dig your hands into the snow, grasping for control, have your gloves ripped off, and slice your hands to bloody smithereens in the ice.

You can scream *STOP!* at the top of your lungs, wave your hands in the air, have your feet slide out from under you, and backward somersault into the snow, wondering how in god's name you didn't end up in the hospital.

There are surely others, but the concussion has stricken them from memory.

IV.

So we told Brickhauser to go ahead and bat-proof the place.

Hold on, he said, studying the front of the house. I think we might have some other hiding places.

He grabbed the garden hose and turned on the water. He sprayed up at the second story, directing the stream behind the window shutters. Out flew bats. First one, then another, and another. Then a bunch.

Holy crap, I said.

Oh my god, stage-whispered Laura.

Then Brickhauser targeted the next shutter. Same thing. Out they came, one after another.

Yep, they're cozied up behind the shutters too, he said.

Hey, can I try that? I asked, taking the hose.

I aimed up at another window shutter and watched the bats fly out. I counted them as they flew, imitating The Count on *Sesame Street*: One, one bat. Two, two bats. Three bats. Four, four bats—

Cut it out, Laura wasn't seeing any humor in this. If we get them out of the attic, what about the ones living behind the shutters? Will they leave too?

Nah, said Batman. No reason for them to leave.

Well, what do we do?

Well, you can scare 'em out every day, like we just did. Maybe after a while they'll get tired of it and just leave. Wouldn't bet on it though.

I had moved onto another window. Yeah, I can just hose 'em out every morning, I said. It was kind of fun.

We're not spraying the house for bats every day, Laura said. She was having no fun.

Well, you can take down the shutters, said Brickhauser, then they'll have no place to stay.

The house is going to look kind of strange without shutters, I said.

The house is going to look kind of strange with nobody in it, said Laura.

All this time, Cesar, the painter, and his helper, Guillermo, were watching the goings-on with detached amusement. They had come outside, probably to breathe, their bodies dripping with sweat from the work of painting inside in the oppressive heat. Every once in a while, they exchanged comments in Spanish, pointing up at the house, but mostly they just watched and chuckled as the bats were flushed from behind the window shutters.

All right, said Brickhauser. My guys'll be here in the morning, and we'll get started.

What time?

About seven thirty, eight.

Can you remove the shutters? asked Laura.

No, we don't do that. You can do it yourself or maybe get a handyman to do it.

Laura looked at me. She was probably thinking back to the fireplace.

We'll ask someone, she said.

What's the matter, I asked in the bedroom darkness, prompted by the tossing and turning.

I can't sleep.

What's wrong? The heat? The paint smell?

Yeah, that too.

What do you mean?

I mean the house is full of bats. We're sleeping in a bat house.

Well, technically, you're *not sleeping* in a bat house, I said.

Don't start.

Look, I said, trying to be reassuring. Nothing's different from yesterday. It's been years and we never even noticed the bats. And tomorrow we'll get it all taken care of. Brickhauser will get rid of the bats, and it'll be done with.

But what about the shutters? There are bats all over the place.

Don't worry. I'll take care of it.

How?

I'll ask someone.

Rising early after a sleepless night, we were waiting for Brickhauser. Even before he arrived, Cesar pulled up in his van with Guillermo, and they started unloading their painting supplies for the day.

Seven thirty in the morning, and it was already hot as hell. They were predicting record high temperatures yet again.

Brickhauser's truck came rattling down the lane with another old pickup not far behind. Our driveway was looking like the parking lot of a construction site. All that was missing was a porta potty.

There you go, boys, he said to his two men. Two skinny guys in jeans and T-shirts with a lot of hair.

Standard stuff, said Brickhauser. Seal it up, and hang the doors.

They began pulling their ladders and rigging from the trucks while Cesar and Guillermo laid out their paint buckets and tools on drop cloths spread out over the driveway like some sort of tradesmen's picnic.

The bat guys set their ladders up against the house, reaching to the roof, then started mixing some concoction in buckets that they would carry in slings wrapped around their shoulders.

Cesar and Guillermo watched for a bit, then began carrying their own stuff into the house to begin their work.

I just stood out by the front door watching the activities, already sweating through my clothes. I couldn't imagine doing such physical work in this heat. I felt a twinge of guilt and a little wimpy. Man, did these guys work hard.

You know what? Laura was standing behind me. We should tell Cesar not to work today. It's just too hot. They're going to get heat stroke. It's inhumane.

Maybe I should tell the bat guys to come back another day too.

Her demeanor turned. Don't you dare let those bat guys leave, she said. I don't care if they fry their lunch on the driveway, they're not going anywhere until the bats are gone.

I caught up to Cesar climbing the stairs, carrying buckets of brushes and other supplies.

Hey, listen, I said, it's really hot. *Muy caliente*. Maybe you don't want to work today. Come back tomorrow. *Mañana*.

Oh no, he said. Work. It's OK.

But there's not even any air-conditioning, I said.

It's good. It's OK. We work.

Then he shouted something in Spanish to Guillermo, and they continued setting up.

I tried, I reported back, but he wants to work.

Well, let him know there's plenty of water in the refrigerator. What are you going to do?

I think maybe I'll go over to Starbucks and work there for a while. It'll be cooler than hanging around here.

Wait a minute. What about the bats?

The bat guys are taking care of the bats.

No, I mean the shutters. You said you'd call someone. We need to get someone here to take down those shutters. Today.

Oh, yeah. Right. I'll see what I can find. I'll call a handyman.

Laura was in no mood for delay.

I went upstairs to the office and pulled up the search engines, *Angie's List*, anything that could help me with window-shutter removal. No matches, unless I wanted to buy window shutters, which I surely did not, not even factory direct at deep online discounts. I tried *handyman* and came across the Honey-Do Man. I left a message. I called the No Job Too Small guy. Left a message. Called the Two Guys With A Truck We Do Anything guys. Left a message. Left a few other messages. Couldn't connect. Laura was not going to be happy.

Well? she said, poking her head in the door.

Nothing yet. I left messages.

You left messages.

I left messages.

I couldn't stand it in there, in that stuffy office. The old window air conditioner was chugging along in vain. I felt sorry for it. It was only getting hotter.

111

I wandered outside, thinking I could make my getaway, when I saw Laura talking to Cesar. She was pointing up at the house, and Cesar was nodding.

Then Cesar was talking to Guillermo, motioning up at the house. Guillermo was nodding, with his hand to his chin.

Sí, sí. OK.

Now Cesar went over to talk to Brickhauser, who was looking up at his men at the top of the ladders, fiddling at the base of the roof.

Cesar was clearly trying to make himself understood, and Brickhauser was doing his best to understand. I sidled over to try to figure out what was going on. Then Laura joined us. It was quite a confab. Cesar talking in heavily accented, limited English, randomly throwing in a Spanish word or two; Brickhauser nodding along, doing his best to understand; me with arms folded, glancing back and forth from one to the other, trying to grasp the situation; and, finally, Laura, who looked at Brickhauser and said matter-of-factly, Oh for god's sake. Can these guys use your ladders to take down the window shutters?

Oh, Brickhauser said. Yeah, I guess. Let my guys get some of the work done here, and then he can use the ladders when we break for lunch.

Laura pointed at Brickhauser while she mimed an eating motion to Cesar, speaking in her best Native American English, slowly and loudly, like that would make a difference.

He eat lunch. You use ladders, she pointed at the ladders. Take down shutters. Now pointing up at the windows. It was turning into charades.

OK, said Cesar, nodding.

When will Cesar and Guillermo eat? I asked her.

When the shutters are down, she said. She had a plan and was into implementation mode.

Are you sure everyone understands? I asked.

I left them a message, she said, and headed back into the house.

Everyone went back to work, while the sun rose higher in the sky and the heat grew more oppressive. It was heat you could chew on. I imagined the grass was about to burst into flames. Brickhauser kept an eye on his men, water-soaked bandanas wrapped around their necks, perched on their ladders, spreading some kind of pasty-looking black stuff along the roofline. Cesar and Guillermo were painting the hallway, sweat pouring from their bodies, leaving drops on the floor. I had to get out of there for a while. I didn't know where Laura was, but I thought it best to make my escape before she found me.

I opened the car door and was struck by a blast of heat. The seats were too hot to sit on. The steering wheel too hot to grip. I reached in and started the car up, opened the windows and turned the air conditioner on full blast. I prayed that Laura wouldn't come out to ask where I was going. I leaned against the car, but it burned, and I quickly jumped back. God, it was hot.

When I was finally able to sit in the car, the dashboard display said the outside temperature was 103. I turned on the radio, and it was all about the heat. They were advising everyone to stay indoors (they didn't live in our house); they said conditions were dangerous for the elderly and small children. They said people with respiratory problems or heart conditions should stay inside and keep cool.

They didn't say anything about painting your hallway or bat-proofing your house.

I escaped to Starbucks for a while, where I got some ice coffee and found a seat where I could pretend to work but actually surfed the web, read the sports pages, and watched my carefully selected stocks plummet as if they were melting in the heat. I was even wearing shorts—and I never wear shorts.

After a while, I got an attack of the guilts and reluctantly felt compelled to go home to see what was going on.

I returned to another confab in the driveway. The Removing of the Bats Committee was in full session. Brickhauser's guys were on the front walkway, fiddling with the ladder rigging to reach the upper windows. Brickhauser was carefully supervising this aspect of the operation, directing the placement of the ladders by moving his hands back and forth, saying, Over. Over. Now the other way. Over. Come back a little. Over. More. OK. That's it.

Caesar shot a rat-a-tat-tat of instructions in Spanish to Guillermo and pointed up at the windows. They talked a bit, then Caesar disappeared into the back of his van. Guillermo followed, sticking his head in the back door. They continued to discuss the situation as Caesar began handing Guillermo stuff from inside. Tools. Some Guillermo hung on his belt, others he handed back while the back-and-forth chatter in Spanish continued. Finally, Guillermo seemed satisfied with his equipment. He had a bunch of stuff in his back pockets and other stuff hanging from his belt. He also held a large crowbar kind of thing in his hand. He walked over and started up the ladder while Caesar watched from the ground, shouting instructions, I guess, the whole time.

I joined Laura while Caesar, Brickhauser, and his boys all came over to stand and watch; a full audience for Guillermo's derring-do.

Hope he can take care of this quickly, I thought. We have a game tonight.

You'd think that with such heat they'd call off the game. But in Littleton, Little League is serious business. The game must go on.

Our very first spring in Littleton, I remember taking Matt through the Little League registration process. Little League has a surprising bureaucratic underpinning, and, in Littleton, this takes on some major overtones. For example, in addition to the standard registration and insurance forms, as the parent of a Little Leaguer you're required to sign a pledge that you won't be disruptive during games and will not make disparaging comments about the players, their supporters, the coaches or the umpires. Violations of this pledge are punishable by a fine of up to $100,000 and possible life imprisonment without parole. This last was a compromise that was the subject of heated debate at a raucous town council meeting. The right-wing Republicans that dominated Littleton politics argued for the death penalty, while a minority of leftist progressives proposed that we shouldn't even keep score. A bipartisan collection of populist libertarians wanted no pledge at all, suggesting that the kids had to learn what real life was like sooner or later.

I'd gone with Matt to his first team practice, the only dad who wasn't a coach. There were a few good athletes and a couple of kids who, shall I say, were just learning the fundamentals. We're talking young kids here, but you know, there were still differences.

Anyway, Coach Anderson gathered the kids around and introduced himself, said he was looking forward to a real good season and a lot of fun and stressed the importance of practice and good sportsmanship. He seemed like a good guy. He didn't look all that athletic himself, but word had it that he was one of the best coaches and that the kids liked playing on his teams. He even got along with the parents.

He introduced his assistant coach, Mr. Headley. Mr. Headley said hi and he was looking forward to working with them and if they ever needed anything to let him know. He also seemed like a good guy and a bit of a scrawny contrast to Anderson.

Then Anderson said that they were supposed to have another assistant coach, but that Mr. Sperling got transferred to Japan by his company, so they would try to find someone else. I noticed he wasn't looking at the kids as he talked.

And that's how I became a Little League coach.

Finally, the talking was done, and Anderson told the kids to run out to whatever position they wanted to play. When the smoke cleared, there were eight kids on the pitcher's mound, four kids at first base, two at shortstop and one in right field. One of the shortstops was a girl.

OK, said Coach Anderson, we're going to have to spread out a little and cover all the positions. What we're going to do is that everyone will work out in the infield and the outfield, and everyone who wants to will get a chance to pitch, one at a time. We also need a couple of catchers. Who wants to give it a try at catcher?

Nothing.

Anyone? Catcher is a really important position; it's like the quarterback of the team. The catcher is like the real boss out there. Who wants to try?

Nothing.

OK, well, we're not going to need a catcher right now anyway. The coaches are going to hit a few to the infield and outfield, and we'll see what we've got. Now, how about if you guys at shortstop and first base spread out around the infield. That's it. Don't worry about the position; just spread out around the infield here. The rest of you run out to left field, and Mr. —

To me, Sorry, what's your name?

Bowman. Steve Bowman.

Mr. Bowman here is going to hit some fly balls to you.

To me again, Uh, that OK? You OK with that?

Sure.

Good.

OK, You guys run out there, and Mr. Bowman's going to hit some fly balls, while Mr. Headley hits ground balls to the infielders. Then, later, we'll switch. Everyone will get a chance. OK, let's go.

I grabbed a bat and a bucket of baseballs and headed for the right-field foul line to hit some fly balls to the kids gathered out in center. The kids were young, their attention spans short. After a few fly balls where the preferred fielding position was placing the glove on top of the head and crouching with a look of horror that a baseball might be somewhere in the vicinity, we decided to focus on the fundamentals. I broke the kids up into pairs to play catch.

One mouthy kid named Billy kept throwing the ball to, at, his partner as hard as he could and then berating him for not catching it. Billy had a Mohawk haircut and two pierced earrings in one ear. I told Billy to take it easy, but he told me we needed to toughen these guys up.

Besides, Billy said, I'm going to be the shortstop, and my dad says that's the leader of the team.

Yeah, well, just take it easy a little. It's only the first day.

Don't you want to win? he challenged.

I didn't need to fight with this kid.

Look, I said, I think you've got the hang of it. Why don't you run in and work with the infielders for now?

OK, he said, these guys are just babies anyway.

I could tell that Billy and I were going to develop one of those deep, long lasting, surrogate father-son relationships, where some day, at his Hall of Fame induction, he would thank me, his first Little League coach, for all my support and guidance, for keeping him on the straight and narrow and for putting him on the path to greatness.

Just get over there, I said.

That left me with one odd kid, Sean, odd in several ways, without a partner. One thing you learn about working with kids, no matter the activity or circumstance, you always end up with one odd kid. One without a partner, where he has to be integrated somehow into the larger group without disruption. Impossible.

OK, Sean. You play three-way catch with these two guys—what are your names?

How come we have to play three way? How come us?

I'm sorry, what's your name again?

Why do we have to be the ones? Let Sean play with those guys over there.

Yeah, let him play with those guys.

Yeah . . . what's your name?

Get out of here, Sean. Go find someone else.

Sean looked up at me. Lost. Out of place. I wanted to ease the awkwardness.

Look, I said, I'm the coach. I say what goes here. Here's what we're going to do. You two guys, whatever your names are—from now on you're Harry and Larry—you two run out there about thirty steps. Sean's going to throw you grounders, and you throw the ball back into Sean like he's the first baseman. Got that? OK, get out there. Here you go, Sean.

I tossed him the ball.

He threw a grounder out toward the other two. It stopped about ten feet short. All three of them just stared at me.

All right. Everybody take a break, I shouted to the whole group. Take a spot on the grass, and catch your breath. I'm going to check in with the other coaches.

But we hardly did anything yet, complained Harry.

Yeah, well, it's just the first day. We need to pace ourselves. I'm going to check with the other coaches on what's next. If you don't want to take a break, you can throw the ball around a little more. I'll be back in a minute.

I walked away but glanced back to see what was going on. They were all sitting around, some lying around, on the grass, chanting something that sounded like nonsense. No one was fighting. I took it as a victory.

Back in the infield, Coach Anderson was conducting an actual practice. He had the kids spread out around the infield while he hit grounders to them. They caught a surprising number of them and attempted to throw them in to a kid who stood next to Anderson with a catcher's mitt. Most of the throws just flew by the catcher into the backstop, and the catcher would sometimes throw down his mitt before running back to pick up the errant baseball. I did notice my old friend Billy between second and third, all serious dirt and grit. He was probably the best athlete on the field. Next to him was the girl. Jennifer. Jenny.

So, what's the story with the girl? I asked Anderson as he continued to hit grounders. Now this was long before girls were commonplace Little Leaguers.

Yeah, Jenny. Nice kid. Good athlete. She's a regionally ranked gymnast in her age group. She wanted to play ball, so they tried to get her to join girls' softball, but she refused. Only wanted to play hardball.

She looks like she can hold her own.

Yep. Very competitive. Fast too.

What's with that kid Billy?

He's got a mouth on him, but he's probably our best player.

Yeah, he told me.

Anderson laughed. So, what's going on with your group out there?

Let's say we've got some challenges. Teamwork is one of them. Then there's the basic ability to catch and throw the ball.

All right. Maybe let's switch groups. Send those guys in here, and I'll send this group out.

OK, uh, where's our other guy, Rich, is it?

Some kind of dinner thing. He'll be back Thursday.

I waved to Matt, who was out by second base, as I headed back out to my troops. I got the barest of acknowledgments with a slight head nod. He was focusing on the ball, the bat, his teammates, the head coach, the dugout, the backstop, the bases—basically, anything but Dad.

As I approached my group of outfielders, who were sprawled across the grass deeply immersed in an analysis of a TV show, I shouted to them in my best upbeat coach's voice.

OK, guys. Let's go. Infield practice. Let's get a move on. Come on, jog on over there, I urged.

They were less than enthusiastic and could best be described as meandering across the field to switch places with the other group, which was coming running toward them. How had Anderson managed to get all the good kids in his group?

OK, let's get out there, I called to my new charges. Let's take some fly balls.

They caught some, they dropped some, but they went after them all. Every time I hit a ball, a chorus of *I got it*s rang out. Even Jenny was in the mix, though I noticed that fly balls weren't her strength, and she still, well, threw like a girl. On the other hand, Billy thought every ball was his and often cut in front of another kid to try to make the catch. I made sure to direct a few toward Matt, and he held his own, but he still wasn't going to pay any special attention to me. They sure were an enthusiastic bunch though.

We went at it for about twenty minutes, having some real fun. Even Billy gave out a *Good catch* every now and then, though he still bullied himself into the picture on nearly every ball. He also issued a disdainful *Come on* when anyone missed.

Our practice was interrupted by a sharp, shrill whistle from Anderson.

He waved his arms at us. Come on in, guys. Hustle up.

My kids took off for home plate where Anderson was gathering the team.

He had them sitting on the infield grass in a rough semicircle while he gave a bit of a pep talk. Good day, good practice. We're gonna have a great season and a lot of fun. If we work hard . . .

I stood off to the side and behind, out of the way, looking over the troops. Matt avoided looking at me, intent on being just one of the team despite being a coach's son. I noticed the competitive Jenny and the obnoxious Billy sitting together.

Well, I thought, if nothing else, we're going to lead the league in earrings.

Little League is a family affair. For practices, parents take turns providing a team snack—chips, cookies and cupcakes were the typical fare. When it was our turn, Laura brought carrot sticks and raisins. Some of the kids were too polite to moan.

It got worse.

The Little League ran a little snack shack to raise money during games, which could last for hours and hours with all the teams. Parents took turns manning the store, selling sodas, hot dogs, candy and the like.

A warning quickly spread through the dugout on certain days: Matt's mom is at the snack shack.

You couldn't blame them. A kid would step up to the little snack bar window with his money in hand and ask for a pack of Twizzlers.

And Laura would say, Don't you think you've had enough candy today? Or, David, I think that's enough soda. Drink water. Or, No, Jason, I'm not giving you one of those disgusting hot dogs. Just wait until dinner. Have a piece of fruit.

After a while, we were not asked to volunteer for the snack shack any more. They were losing money.

Coaching Little League is an interesting experience. You hear a lot of horror stories about interfering, disruptive, argumentative or obnoxious parents, but we really didn't have much of that. Parents sat in the stands and rooted on their kids as well as the others. All very supportive.

Control is naturally a big problem for pitchers that young. Our age group was the first year that the kids pitched for themselves, resulting in a lot of very long games. Very, very long games. Lots of walks. But every time the pitcher threw a pitch, and the umpire yelled *Ball*, a chorus rose from the parents in the stands on the batter's side: *Good eye, good eye!*

The Good-Eye League.

Strikeouts elicited *Attaboys* from the pitcher's-side parents, and *Don't worry you'll get him next time* from the batter's. Every error was a *Good try*. Every dropped fly ball was a *Tough chance*. Every hit was a *Wow*. Every run evoked a standing ovation. Rarely did they criticize an umpire, and a kid's complaint to his parents in the stands about anything was invariably met with *Listen to Coach Anderson*.

An optional name, the Positive-Reinforcement League.

We weren't very good, but, then, neither was anyone else. The key to success in the lower levels of Little League is catching the ball. There are about 178 errors per game and about 84 walks. If your team can catch the ball and actually get someone out, you're going to be way ahead. We couldn't quite manage that. If we managed to catch a ground ball, the fielder would invariably launch it well over the head of the first baseman, into the stands or the parking lot. On the other hand, the attempt at a throw might well be driven straight into the ground, a few feet from the fielder. If the ball did arrive at the first baseman, it was about fifty-fifty it would be caught versus hitting him in the chest or bouncing out of his glove.

Fly balls were a circus. Any fly ball that was caught was cause for loud and lengthy celebration. An outfielder that caught a fly ball to end an inning after, say, eleven runs had scored, might be surrounded by his teammates, who would run out to greet him and carry him off the field on their shoulders.

Aside from obnoxious Billy, our best athlete was probably Jenny, except that she couldn't really hit. She was fast and fearless but just awkward with a bat in her hands. I had an idea.

One day during practice, I took her out to the outfield, pitched to her and taught her to bunt. She took to it in no time.

For the rest of the season, every time she came up to bat she bunted. Nine out of ten times the fielders would mess up the play, overrun the ball, throw it away, drop it, or field it too slowly. The speedy Jenny would be safe at first and, usually, just keep going. She'd hit second base ahead of a dropped throw and head for third. She was so fast that the fielders panicked. More often than not, she'd round the bases. The only thing that stopped her was if slower boys were on the bases in front of her. Jenny was our secret weapon, our scoring machine. We would ride her ponytails to the playoffs.

We were all excited to be in the playoffs, but it wasn't going well. Our star pitcher (Anderson's son) gave up seven runs on five walks, several errors and, charitably, a hit in the top of the first inning. Fortunately, we got out of the inning when one of the kids on the other team was caught between first and second on an odd play that defies explanation. All I can tell you is with one out, a ground ball was hit to our second baseman who dropped it, picked it up, dropped it, picked it up and threw a little short of first base where our first baseman came off the bag to get the ball and then ran back to first base to narrowly beat the runner who, apparently, had stopped just a few feet up the baseline to watch our second baseman wrestle with the baseball. Meanwhile, the aforesaid runner from first base stopped to watch the proceedings as well. The second baseman, who could have simply stepped on second base to record an out, ultimately decided, as I said, to hoist the ball toward first base, while the runner stopped to watch. When our first baseman ran back to first with the retrieved baseball, and stepped on first (an out!), he was obviously proud of himself and made quite a show of his fielding prowess, while his teammates and coaches in the dugout were yelling at him to tag the kid who, for reasons unknown, was still standing midway between first and second. The calls from the dugout grew to screams while the first baseman looked confused. Obnoxious Billy, our shortstop, was standing on second base yelling, Throw it! Throw it, you dope. Throw it!

Cut it out, Billy, called Coach Anderson. There's no need for that.

Finally, our pitcher yelled at the first baseman, Give it here. The embattled and confused first baseman threw it to him, and our pitcher walked (walked!) over to the kid standing (yes, still standing) between first and second and tagged him for a double play. We were out of the inning.

Our fans in the stands exploded with a *way-to-go* chorus and raucous applause.

The third base coach wrapped his arm around the shoulder of his confused base runner with a That's OK, Sean; you were almost safe, and led him off the field.

We knew we'd narrow the gap almost immediately. Jenny was our leadoff hitter. By now, everyone knew what was coming. She picked out a pitch, bunted it toward third base, and took off. She never slowed down as the ball was hurled over the head of the first baseman into right field, then into the dirt in front of the third baseman long after Jenny had rounded the bag and crossed home plate, to be followed a few seconds later by the ball flying into the backstop over the head of the ducking umpire. High fives all 'round in the dugout.

After Jenny's expected, ahem, homerun, the game settled into the usual rhythm. Lots of balls (*Good eye!*), lots of errors (*Nice try!*), and strikeouts with kids swinging at pitches well over their heads (*You'll get 'em next time!*).

We'd played four innings and had been out there for two hours. I'm not sure what the score was at that point—12 to 9? 15 to 10? I don't know, something like that.

Anderson called Headley and me over for, I imagined, a strategy consultation.

Look, he said, I've got to leave in about ten minutes. A thing with my in-laws. George, you take over, and I'll give you a call later to see how things went.

So Headley was now managing the team. Our guys finished their at bats, and we took the field with Danny

Headley now pitching and Alex Anderson moving to first base.

Danny was a good kid. A little quieter than some of the others but still an enthusiastic part of the group. He liked playing the outfield and catching high flies. His father, though, wanted him to pitch. Danny didn't really like pitching; he preferred the outfield where there was plenty of room between him and a batted baseball. With each pitch he threw, he kind of winced and ducked, expecting the ball to be hit back at him. It made for a lot of balls out of the strike zone. A lot. Whenever Danny pitched, opposing coaches told their weaker hitters not to swing, Just wait and take your base. Lots of *Good eye*s.

Poor Danny. I felt for the kid, but his father kept egging him on: Come on there, Danny. Find the plate. No hitter up there.

After a while, I stepped to Headley's side.

You know, Danny's arm looks kind of tired out there. Maybe we should get him into the outfield so he can rest his arm for the next game.

Yeah, but then what? Anderson's already pitched, and Billy pitched on Tuesday, so he's not allowed.

Matt can throw strikes. Let's put him out there. I bet it'll calm things down.

Matt?

Yeah.

You mean your kid, Matt?

Yeah. Believe me, he'll throw strikes.

But then what do we do for catcher?

Put Billy back there.

Billy? No, we need him at short. He's our best player.

No, not him. The other Billy.

What other Billy?

Billy Ho.

Who?

Ho.

Ho?

Yeah, Ho.

Headley looked down the bench where an Asian kid sat mesmerized by something in the parking lot.

Hey, Ho, called Headley.

No response.

Ho! Hey, Ho! Billy Ho!

Yeah? Billy Ho looked over.

Come over here. Time, Ump, Headley called across the diamond.

C'mere, Matt.

OK, Matt, give the gear to Ho here. He's going to catch. You're pitching.

Headley walked out to the mound and sent Danny out to left field, told Jenny, who was the left fielder and didn't really have much to do out there anyway, to move to right, and waved our right fielder into the dugout.

None of the kids seemed to mind.

Move it along, said the ump. We only got about seven hours of daylight left.

Matt took the mound and, predictably, threw strikes. All those early evenings on an empty field at the local high school paid off. Matt would pitch, and I'd call balls and strikes as I crouched behind the plate to catch.

Throw strikes, Matt. Nothing but strikes. Attaboy. Throw it up there. Let 'em hit it if they can. Throw strikes. Nothing for free. Make 'em hit their way on. Nothing but strikes. Throw strikes.

He must have wanted to kill me.

But there he was, throwing strikes over the next couple of innings. No more walks. Strikeouts. Ground balls; some caught.

Jeez, I should've put this kid in at the beginning, said Headley, leaning up against the dugout fence.

I didn't say a thing.

Somehow, we got to the last inning. Game tied 23–23 or something like that. I may be exaggerating. It might have been 21–21. We had last licks.

Obnoxious Billy led off with a walk, then somehow ended up on third on a slow, pretty much accidental ground ball toward first base by Larry or Harry, not sure which. I was coaching third base and already knew what Billy was thinking.

I'm stealing home.

There's nobody out. Just stay there, I said.

Uh-uh. I'm stealing home.

Every kid in the league who reached third base wanted to steal home. Most tried. To be honest, they were often safe. Ironically, catchers were often the worst catchers on the team.

But this was different. We had our chance here to win this thing. Nobody out. Guy on third. No reason to risk a steal now.

I'm stealing on the next pitch.

Stay there, I said.

I'm going.

On the next pitch, he started home but slipped and fell and had to scramble back to the base. Good thing. The catcher caught the ball, and he would have been dead.

I'm stealing on the next pitch.

Stay there.

I'm going.

The situation called for sound baseball strategy.

On the next pitch, Billy took off but stopped short, his feet flying into the air and flailing about like a cartoon character.

My hand was wrapped around the back of his belt. He wasn't going anywhere.

Hey!

Hey, what?

Let go!

Let go of what?

Let go!

I held my hands wide. Let go of what?

You were holding me.

I don't know what you're talking about. Now heads up. I nodded toward the mound. Next pitch.

Ground ball to second base, caught but heaved well over the head of the first baseman into the parking lot.

Billy scores! We win! Jumping and shouting on the field! High fives all 'round. Hugs and chest bumps. Rejoicing! Lots of positive reinforcement from the sidelines.

It was the highlight of my baseball career.

I think I saw Billy guzzling a beer.

V.

So the bunch of us stood in the driveway watching Guillermo climb the ladder to take down the shutters. Laura was cheerleader and coach. Cesar offered what I took to be encouraging words to Guillermo in Spanish, and I stood, the observer, secure in the knowledge that something was going to go wrong.

As Guillermo climbed the ladder, Brickhauser, clearly in control of the situation, took the hose and yelled to Guillermo that he would shoot the water up at the shutters to make sure there were no bats remaining. Cesar shouted in Spanish, presumably to explain to Guillermo why he was about to be hosed.

Guillermo reached the top of the ladder and fumbled at his belt to grab a tool, then nodded down at Brickhauser, who aimed the nozzle and shot a stream of water up behind the first shutter. Even though we knew what could be coming, we were still startled to see a bat fly out from behind. Guillermo flinched and stuttered a little on the ladder, while we all caught our breath. But he steadied himself and gingerly leaned over to begin detaching the window shutter. The crowd was quiet with nervous anticipation as Guillermo slowly and carefully executed his operation, working with one hand while hanging onto the ladder with the other. Then, balancing precariously, he leaned across to pull the shutter away from the house. Laura and Brickhauser nodded their heads, both appreciative of a good job. Cesar stood with his arms folded across his chest, expecting nothing less than a good work effort. The air was still, not a hint of breeze.

AAIIII! DIOS MIO! Guillermo's blood curdling scream broke the silence.

AAAAIIIIIIIII! AAAAIIIIIIII! AAAIIIIIII! he shrieked, waving the air madly with one hand while holding onto the ladder for dear life.

AAAIIIII! AAAIIII! He wrapped an arm around his head.

AAAIIIII! DIOS MIO! AAAIIII!

And that's how we found the bees.

The shutter dropped to the ground, and Guillermo virtually slid down the ladder, waving at bees with one hand as he landed, screaming in Spanish with Cesar yelling back. Where the shutter had been was now a blank outline next to the window, like the body drawing at a murder scene. There were big stains and splotches all over the newly exposed space. Bees' nests. With angry bees swarming all over.

Shit, said Brickhauser.

Man, said one of his guys.

Brutal, said the other.

Guillermo continued his high-pitched, frantic rant in Spanish while Cesar attempted to calm him down.

Guillermo kept pointing up at the windows; Cesar put his hands out front of him, palms down—take it easy, take it easy, I guessed.

After a few minutes, Guillermo calmed down to a few word spurts at a time but still breathing heavily as the incident began to subside.

Brickhauser sprayed up at the beehives and a lot of the stuff fell apart, and the debris came dropping to the ground.

Lots of those nests are dead, said Brickhauser in cool appraisal, but not all of 'em.

Laura turned to Cesar, a little panicked, pleading.

You're still going to be able to take down the shutters, right?

Cesar reopened the dialogue with Guillermo, who, so far as I could tell, said something like, No, no, no, no—with some added, more colorful language, I suspected.

Cesar talked a little bit more.

Guillermo said something like, No, no, no, no. He shook his head for emphasis, which made the translation a bit easier.

Laura talked quietly, slowly and desperately to Cesar. I understand it's a problem, a very hard job. Thank you for doing this. *Muchas gracias*. How can we help? We can pay more.

Cesar nodded and turned again to Guillermo and said, if I may offer my guess at a rough translation, something like, Let's do this. The lady's going to pay big bucks.

Now Cesar ignored me completely. He went over to Laura and started talking with her in a low voice that I couldn't make out. The two of them wandered up the driveway a bit, Cesar talking and Laura nodding. They started walking back toward us, and all I could make out was Laura saying OK.

Cesar and Guillermo went over to their van and disappeared inside. You could see the truck rocking as they dug through their gear and cans of old paint.

What are they doing? I asked Laura

Getting ready, she said.

Ready?

Battle gear.

After a few minutes, Cesar and Guillermo emerged from the truck carrying a bundle of clothes and a bunch of rags. They stood on the driveway, and Guillermo pulled a white painter's coverall over his shorts and T-shirt, and Cesar wrapped the rags around Guillermo's neck and head, leaving only a small slit for his eyes. Then Guillermo pulled on a pair of thick, white gloves.

The Paint Mummy. I imagined Guillermo was vaporizing inside his bee suit, that before he climbed the ladder he'd simply melt right there in the garden, leaving a steaming stack of coveralls and rags like the wicked witch of Oz.

But he moved the ladder over to the next shutter and climbed up slowly. When he got to the top, however, he realized his tools were hanging from his pockets and belt inside the coveralls. This made for an awkward little dance atop the ladder that had us all on edge, watching a high-wire act.

AND NOW, THE GREAT GUILLERMO WILL PERFORM AN UNPRECEDENTED DEATH-DEFYING FEAT OF SKILL AND COURAGE. HE WILL ATTEMPT—ATTEMPT!—TO DETACH A WINDOW

SHUTTER WHILE BALANCING PRECARIOUSLY HIGH ABOVE THE EARTH ON NOTHING MORE THAN A WORKMAN'S LADDER, WITHOUT A NET BELOW, WHILE BEING VICIOUSLY AND RELENTLESSLY ATTACKED BY THOUSANDS OF SWARMING, STINGING, MAN-EATING BEES! BEHOLD, THE GREAT GUILLERMO!

Guillermo looked down. Brickhauser flooded the shutter, and Guillermo set to work to detach it. Guillermo let go the second shutter and dropped it to the ground, revealing another bunch of bees' nests. He swatted the swarm away with one hand, holding onto the ladder for dear life with the other and, as quickly as he could gather his wits, nearly slid back down the ladder to safety. There were bees flying everywhere, and the crowd was restless, ducking and swatting themselves.

All of this, of course, complicated the task of finishing the bat sealing and hanging the bat doors. Brickhauser and his bat crew had been at the house for quite a while now as the shutter and bee show dragged on. We were well past lunch, and Brickhauser's guys were on down time.

Look, Brickhauser said to me, without taking his eyes off the upper windows, my guys have been here quite a while, and we're not getting anything done. And they can't go up there again until we get rid of those bees' nests. Thing is, if we're stuck here, we can't work anywhere else. So, if we're going to hang around and get this mess cleaned up, I'm going to have to charge you more.

Of course.

I mean, we can't be hanging around here without doing anything and not get paid.

I understand.

Have to charge you another seventygrillion dollars.

Uh-huh.

OK, then. When your guy here finishes taking down those shutters, we'll wash down the rest of the house and get those bees nests out of there. Then, after a while, when the bees disperse, we can get back up there and get the job done.

Sure.

All right then.

So Guillermo set to work removing the shutters. Suited up in his anti-bee outfit, he gingerly spent the next couple of hours climbing up and down, moving window to window, battling the bees and dropping the shutters to the ground. When the last of the shutters was removed, the whole crew stood in the driveway, silently surveying the front of the house. Brickhauser took the hose and sprayed the blotchy remains of the old beehives where the shutters had been.

I watched the water soak the house and do an ineffective job of cleaning, then turned to Laura and said quietly, Probably should have closed those windows.

One of the charms of life in the woods is the occasional power outage. The power lines in Littleton all run above ground, through the trees and, in our case, through the dense woods. A major storm, or high winds, or, hell, a stiff breeze, can lead to falling branches, felled trees and disrupted power lines.

As a matter of fact, when we first went house hunting in Connecticut, we had never heard of Littleton. On our way to see a house in another town one day, we were driving through this lovely area and wondered aloud where we were. We stopped in the little town center and learned we were driving through Littleton. Had never heard of the place. Didn't know it existed. Several months later, back in The City, the day after we had come to agreement to buy our house, we were watching the local evening news. The main story was about some violent storms that had passed through

Connecticut, raising all sorts of havoc and creating power outages. And there, on the screen, below images of downed trees, crushed cars and flooded roadbeds, with the reporter's voiceover talking about the thousands of homes without electricity, was the caption Littleton, CT.

Our new hometown was famous.

Like anywhere else, a power outage in Littleton brings the usual inconveniences. No TV, no lights, no air conditioners, no electric range or oven, melted ice cream and spoiled food in the refrigerator. But out in the woods, powerlessness presented some added, unsavory challenges. Back in the woods, we don't have town water or sewage. We have a well and a septic system. No power, no well pump, no water. No water, no faucets, no showers, no toilets. A power outage of any duration really stinks—in so many ways.

At the first sign that we might lose power, that is, whenever there was a rustling in the trees, we hoarded bottled water and filled buckets and pots with water for the toilet. We filled the bathtubs with ice. We showered and shampooed. We collected candles and matches. We stockpiled peanut butter. We ate ice cream. We went to the bathroom.

When an outage finally, inevitably, came, we suffered through the first few hours—or minutes—hoping it would be short lived, that any second the lights would burst on, that we could breathe more easily, knowing that we'd dodged a bullet. But there were those times when the darkness just continued, on and on, into the night. We rationed phone use to preserve battery life, but we repeatedly called the local power company to listen to the recording: *We are aware of a power outage in your area, and we are doing our best to restore power as quickly as possible. Our crews have been dispatched throughout the affected area. We expect your power to be restored by . . .* But too often we'd hear: *We are aware of a power outage in your area, and we don't have a clue when it will be restored. You're pretty much on your own. Have a nice day.*

We'd access the Internet through the cellular network, where the power company's consumer friendly, service-oriented website would show how many customers were without power in each town. We watched the numbers for Littleton go up instead of down. We'd watch them go down and then back up. We'd call again. And again. The lack of information could drive you crazy.

I'm going out to have a look around.

Why? What are you going to do?

I don't know. At least I can see if there are crews working out there, see what's going on.

Well, don't do anything stupid.

I'll keep that in mind.

I'd drive around, frequently brought to a halt on roads that were blocked by fallen trees, occasionally coming upon a mass tangle of downed wires and mangled branches. Sometimes it was obvious it would take days to fix, clear the trees, get the wires back up and working. It made me nuts with frustration. I wanted the governor to call out the National Guard, the president to call in the Marines. I wanted rock stars to stage a benefit concert, complete with T-shirts bearing a clever logo and a call-in number at the bottom of the TV screen for everyone to donate. I wanted a Facebook and Twitter storm. I wanted something done!

The year after the summer of the bats, we were out for six days. We showered at friends' houses and lived on sandwiches from a local store that had a generator. About three days in, we realized that the rest of the town was up and running and back to normal. In our neck of the woods, the calendar was turned back to 1900. We suffered through that outage, and, wouldn't you know it, just three weeks later another big storm hit and again we had widespread outages. Same drill. We were drained, fed up. The whole town was out. It hit on a Saturday. I was due in Las Vegas for a business meeting on Monday.

Look, I can stay if you want.

No. There's nothing you can do here. You may as well go.

Are you sure you'll be all right?

Sure, what can happen? I'll be fine. I'll sit here with my candles and my book and the dog. The power will be back on soon.

OK, if you're sure.

Sunday afternoon I took a car to the airport. I kept texting out of guilt, but Laura told me to stop because it was using up the battery on her phone, and she didn't want to keep running out to the car to charge it, and, besides, it was starting to use up gas. I said I'd call when I got to Vegas.

Long taxi lines, traffic, and longer lines still at the hotel check-in. But who was I to complain?

I chatted up the perky, smiling desk clerk, noticed her name badge and lied that I was from the same town as she, and asked if she could find me a good room. Life on the road teaches you things.

How about an upgrade to a suite?

Well, that'd be great, I said.

She started clicking away on her keyboard. And clicking some more. And some more.

Finally, she looked up in triumph. I've got a beautiful suite on the twenty-third floor overlooking the fountains. It's really nice. You'll love it.

You know, I'm not really from the same home town. I was just joking.

Well, you seem nice. Keep the suite anyway.

I did visit there once.

Next.

It was a beautiful suite. All decked out with, well, everything, including a vast wall of windows with electrically operated drapes that offered a fantastic view of the lights of Las Vegas and the dancing waters of the Bellagio below. Nice.

It was late by eastern time, so I unpacked and took care of a few things, then called Laura.

I'm here. How's it going?

Power's still out. They don't know when it will come back.

What are you doing? Are you OK?

Well, I'm sitting here, wrapped in a blanket with the dog snoring next to me. I've got a candle, and I'm trying to read my book. It's dark and chilly. I had half a turkey sandwich from the deli for dinner and—

Hang on a minute. Room service is at the door.

I can't believe you're in Las Vegas.

Hey—you said I should go.

I know but—

And they gave me a very nice suite. It's beautiful.

How wonderful.

The sarcasm was thick.

Listen, I said, someday we'll look back on this, and it will all be funny.

Not yet.

She greeted me at the door when I got home.

Anything?

Power's back.

Great.

We're getting a generator.

Oh?

Oh yes. Tomorrow you're calling and getting a generator installed. I'm not going through this again.

There was absolutely no suitable response other than OK.

It was November. Two storms had hit, three weeks apart, producing widespread outages across the entire region. I did some lookups and called a local generator company. Left a message.

Called another company. Left a message.

Called the first company again. Left a message.

When will the generator be installed?

I called a couple of places and left messages. Waiting for them to get back to me.

How long are you going to wait?

If I don't hear back, I'll call again tomorrow.

Left a message.

Called the other. Left a message.

Then I called again, and this time hit *8* for emergency service.

Service.

Hello, I'm in Littleton, and I need to get a generator installed. I've left a number of messages, but no one has returned my calls.

Are you a current customer?

No. I'm trying to be a current customer. I need to get a generator installed.

Well, this line is for emergency service. For a new installation, you have to talk to sales.

I've been trying to talk to sales, but I can't get sales.

Well, this line is for emergencies.

This is an emergency. It's a matter of life and death.

What do you mean?

If I don't get a generator, my wife is going to kill me.

I'll transfer you to sales.

Yesterday, all my troubles seemed so far away . . .

Forty minutes later, a guy picked up.

Eastern Generator.

Yes, I want to get a generator installed.

Yeah, where are you?

Littleton.

OK. We can add you to the list. Right now we're making appointments for April.

April?!

Yeah. We're at the third week in April. I've got the morning of the twenty-fourth open. We'll call you the day before to confirm.

Whoa. Wait, wait. I don't know anything about these things. I'm not sure what to get, how it gets installed. Nothing.

Our sales guy will go over everything when he gets out there. He'll survey the site. Go over your options. He'll set you up with the best configuration.

In late April? When would the generator be installed?

Well, you get everything sorted out with the sales rep, sign the contract, and make your deposit—probably get installed by June. July latest.

This was not going to go over well. I thought about hitting *8* for emergency service again.

Well, should I put you down for the twenty-fourth?

April?

Yeah, April 24. Do you want the appointment or not?

Yeah, sure, put me down.

You got it.

Let me ask you. If there's a cancellation—

He'd hung up.

I envisioned telling Laura we'd have the generator in June. July latest.

I needed to generate another solution.

Back online, searching for a generator. Companies in the Midwest had them available to ship. A company in Oregon guaranteed delivery within the week. I even came across a company in Estonia, *Delivery to U.S. available*, but the fine print didn't appear on the English-page version. Besides, I didn't know anything about generators. I imagined a truck pulling into the driveway, unloading a big box of a thing, then pulling away. I wasn't going to know what the hell to do with it. And, if I somehow figured it out, who would I call if something went wrong, if there was a part missing, if something needed to be fixed? I needed someone nearby, someone in the general vicinity of the northeastern United States.

Finally, I saw an ad for generators from a local hardware store a few towns over. I made the call.

Yes, we have generators.

All right! How do I go about getting one installed?

Well, how big is your house, and what do you want the generator to do?

I want it to turn on when we lose power. I don't want to go through one of those power outages again.

Well, what you got to do is have an electrician come out and survey the house. Then we can decide what size and get it out to you. But you got to get all the work done. Do you have gas?

That seemed like an awfully personal question.

Not at the moment, I answered, puzzled.

Well, if you don't have gas, you're going to need a propane tank.

Do you sell propane tanks?

No. You got to get that from the fuel company.

Silly me, I thought. I figured you called a generator guy, he installed a generator, life went on. But, no. This was just the beginning. It started a saga involving a whole bunch of new guys—several of which turned out to be, finally, women. As a matter of fact, the person I talked to at the hardware store sounded like a pretty big guy, but it turned out to be a woman. I'll bet Rusty could kick my ass.

The next days brought an avalanche of activities, tasks, people, questions and building-code requirements. It was dizzying, and I was spinning out of control. It felt like an endless swarm of bees, mosquitos, fleas and flies were buzzing about my head. I was losing it: The electrician and his assistant came out to the house and told me what kind of generator I'd need, which was scary, along with something called a passive transfer switch, which was scarier still. But we looked OK with the existing circuits, which was a relief, depending on how much of the house I wanted to power, and they didn't recommend including the washer/dryer or the garage or extra things because they'd just use up fuel anyway and the only appliance you should really power up is the refrigerator. And we'll have to find a spot for the generator, because it has to be at least twelve horizontal feet from any window or door or vent or other opening, and five vertical feet too, and you need it on level ground, and dig a trench from the generator to the propane tank—and what the hell is a horizontal foot? And what size tank are you getting, probably 120 gallon, right? (Sure, I guess. Why not?). That'll keep you going for a few days at least, depending on how much power you use, but talk to the propane guys. The propane guy, er, woman, came out and surveyed the property to locate the propane tank and show us where we had to dig the trench. And the propane tank had to be five horizontal feet from any opening, and you had to do that because the inspectors would come to make sure it was all up to code.

It was exhausting and intimidating. At this point I was seriously thinking of moving to Las Vegas.

The days passed into December. Merry effing Christmas. Freezing-ass cold, with the ground hard as rock. I called the summer lawn guy—different from the landscape guy or the tree guy—but his daughter answered and said he was in Brazil for the winter. So I found another lawn guy who was still in town on account of he also did snow removal—if I needed a plow guy—which, of course, I didn't (I had Mitch The Ineffectual Plow Guy). Anyway, right now I just needed the trench dug for a gas line from the propane tank to the generator.

Two mountain men unloaded a big crate from the back of a truck and set it in the middle of the driveway. Then they left. For all I knew an elephant could have walked out of that crate. The installation people came and pointed out that there was no flat ground where I wanted to put the generator. I needed a concrete slab. Then they left.

I didn't know any concrete-slab guys. The new lawn guy (now, the trench guy) did, so he called a friend, and he said it might be hard to mix the concrete in the cold, but he would see what he could do. And he did. So the new slab guy laid down a concrete slab, and then I called the generator-installation guys to come back, and, after pleading, beseeching and offering an outright bribe, they returned and hauled the generator out back and placed it on the slab. Then they left.

Then the electrician came out to install the panel and hook up the generator and the transfer switch. And the propane guy, er, woman, had a tank sent out, and then the propane-tank-installer guys came out and placed the tank but said the trench wasn't deep enough and that it couldn't have such sharp corners. So the lawn guy (I mean, trench guy) sent his guys out again, and they struggled with the hard ground to make the trench deeper and make a nice sweeping curve around the corner of the house. Then the propane guys came back and hooked the lines up and ran them to the generator, and the electrician guys came back and tested the hookup and the generator and then told me the town building inspector had to come out to see the site and make sure everything was up to code before they could issue the certificate.

Everyone seemed to be having a good old time. The generator business was good. Surely boat sales were up.

I took up deep breathing at the local Y, chanted Om, and called the town hall to talk to the buildings department, but they said that the planning and zoning department had to update their maps before they could inspect it, and I should have done that before any work was done to make sure it was all OK, but maybe it would be OK anyway. So I went down to town hall to the planning and zoning department where I pleaded on bended knee with Willy, the weathered planning and zoning guy, who pulled an old map of the property and made a copy and asked me to sketch in where the generator and propane tank were going to be installed. Then he asked me for my address again, which was a little odd, since we were already looking at the map. When I pointed this out Willy stared into my eyes for a minute, then said something like, Oh. Then he turned his attention back to the map we'd been looking at and said it might be a little close to the building, which, I thought, could be a real problem since I already had the slab and the generator and propane tank and the trench and the lines and electrical hookup, and if I had to move the generator, well, I just don't know, and I was fast running out of valium.

But Willy agreed to send the building guy out, and asked me for the address again, which I wrote down for him. So the building guy came, except that he was late and explained that he had the wrong address, but he looked at the installation and said it just made it. And the trench got filled in, and everything was hunky-dory, and the propane tank got delivered, and I signed a maintenance contract with the generator guys, and the electrician came out to give everything one final test.

For the grand finale, the electrician and I—the real guy, not the assistant—stood in the basement, and the electrician flipped some switch and the lights went out, and we stood in utter blackness for what seemed like an eternity. Then, after about thirty seconds, says he, the lights came back on. I ran up and checked all the rooms in the house. The power was on. It was a miracle. Back down in the basement, he showed me a simulation of the power coming back on, and how the main power kicked in again automatically while the generator turned off. Power off, power on, everything working, and I didn't have to lift a finger. It was a thing of beauty.

It cost a fortune, not to mention a heap of aggravation, but Laura was happy and I was a hero. I couldn't wait for the next power outage.

That was six years ago. Still waiting.

It was a couple of months after we had the generator installed that I had a melt-down one cold, cloudy February day. Eight inches of milky-white, ice-crusted snow covered the ground. The sharp cold whipped through my jacketless arms, hands buried in my pants pockets, shoulders scrunched up around my ears, as I surveyed the white expanse from the back deck. Bitter memories of power outages and the generator fiasco bubbled up within me, creating an outsized rumbling irritation. The last bunch of characters that had been running in and out of our lives paraded through my mind, along with visions of a mountainous stack of bills and invoices. The electrician, the generator salesman, the propane lady, the planning and zoning inspector, the buildings department lady, Willy, the winter version of the landscape guys, the concrete guys. It seemed endless, and I was fed up. I looked over at the woodpile and noticed just a few remaining logs sitting at the bottom of the rack. Great. Now I had to call the firewood guy. I scanned the property, steely eyed, silently cursing this life in the woods—years of fighting the elements and the land, battling wildlife, and personally fueling the local economy. The resentment rose and caught in my throat. I yearned for the simple city life, where most problems could be delegated to the handyman or the doorman, where most needs were met by an easy stroll up the block and satisfactorily ended with a quick slice from the corner pizza joint. Over at one end of the property, close to the fieldstone wall, a bunch of large logs lay lifelessly strewn about the edge of the lawn, the residue of a couple of trees we had taken down the previous fall. There they lay. My eyes rose to the tops of the winter-bare trees overhead, rattling in the wind, dark scraggly limbs against a slate gray sky. I looked down at the logs and over at the empty wood rack again. And at the logs, and the trees. Everything began to spin, and then the earth slowed as clarity poked through my skull. A sneer formed at my lips. A venomous guttural laugh rose from my throat. The trees, the logs, the trees, the logs.

Hell, I thought. I may have to pay for every other damn thing around here, but one thing I sure don't have to pay for is firewood. I've got a whole friggin' forest of firewood!

All I had to do was turn those trees into fireplace logs. Just like the pioneers. They built whole houses. I could surely cut up a few logs. All I needed was a good axe.

Off to Home-Is-Us.

There was a confusing array of sharp-edged, long handled axe-like tools displayed on a large rack at the end of an aisle of shelves. The little descriptive pricing cards identified various sizes and styles. Jeez. I thought an axe was an axe.

Can I help you?

In disbelief, I ground my fists into my eyes, seeing before me an orange-aproned, pleasant guy with a friendly beard who was offering assistance.

Yeah, thanks, I said, a little startled. I need to split some wood. Split logs into firewood. I thought I just needed an axe, but I'm a little confused here.

What kind of logs are you going to be splitting? Small logs that need to be split in two, or something bigger?

Nah. Big fat logs. We cut down a couple of trees, and the pieces of trunk are lying all over the lawn. I want to cut them up for firewood.

By hand?

Well, yeah, I guess. How else?

Well, you could get a gas-powered splitter. Make the whole job a lot easier—and faster.

Hmm. What does one of those things run?

Home use? They go for a few hundred dollars and up. You want to see them?

No, no. I want to do this by hand, I said, thinking I needed to pick up a red-checkered flannel shirt, too.

So what's the right thing here, I asked, pointing to the rack of treacherous-looking implements of destruction.

Well, how big are these logs of yours? Show me.

I put my arms out in front of me so that anyone walking by would have thought I was describing how big I expected to get in my pregnancy.

Oh, sizeable. Well, OK, I think you want a maul.

A maul?

Yeah, a splitting maul. Look here. See, an axe has a light, sharp, narrow head. It's for cutting smaller pieces, or you can spend the day chopping down a small tree. Then you have your splitting axe, he said, moving on. A little heavier, bit duller blade, and a little wider for splitting smaller pieces of wood, usually in two. For the logs you want to split, probably in four or more sections, you're gonna want something heftier to do the job. A maul. Lookit here. It's longer, got a heavy head, dull blade. You swing that sucker down onto the log, and it's going to tear right through the wood fibers and give you a nice cut. Nice fire-size logs. That's what you want. A maul.

A maul. I loved the sound of it. He handed one over. I tested its weight in the air and ran my hand along the long, silky, pale wood handle. I ran my thumb along the thick, dull, heavy iron blade. Come to Daddy. This is what I want. A maul. A maul sounded like it could do some real damage. This was a thing. A maul. Bring it on.

Yeah, I said. I need a maul.

Back at home, I couldn't wait to get started. I pulled my maul from the car and headed right out back to begin my life as a woodsman. I sized up the scene and realized I needed some kind of platform to set the logs on for splitting. There was a large, clean-cut stump from one of the trees we'd taken down that seemed like it would serve pretty well. I did notice a bit of a problem in that this whole little area was on an incline, making the angles and footing a little tricky, but I was eager to get started. I also noticed that as I stomped around this little section of lawn near the stump on the hill, the snow packed down under my feet and turned the ground a little slicker, a little icier. I kept slipping in place. One final problem was that I didn't know what the hell I was doing. How do you split logs, anyway?

Well, I thought, you learn by doing. If things went right, I might just build a little log cabin right there on the property. I cannot tell a lie: I damn sure *did* chop down that cherry tree.

I picked out a moderately sized log, hoisted it up, carried it over, slipping here and there, and stood it straight up on the stump. There we go. Where'd I put the maul? There, over by the logs. I went to retrieve the maul, slipped and fell backward into the snow. I pulled the maul from where it lay in the snow and headed back up the little hill to my stump, again slipping and sliding along the way. The ground around the stump was getting smoother and more slippery, a wet, milky slick of ice. This should have been a warning. Nevertheless, I maneuvered myself around to stand on the high side of the stump, but I kept sliding forward into the stump so that I couldn't maintain the right swinging distance. This position clearly wasn't working, so I shifted around to the low side. Now I started sliding away from the stump, so that I couldn't reach it with the maul. OK, I thought. Let me approach this thing from the side, but that didn't work either—too awkward with one foot uphill and one down. Hey, I was a smart guy. I could figure this out. I stood thinking.

Screw it. Let's just do this.

I positioned myself below the stump and immediately felt myself sliding away. I tentatively moved back up the incline, bent over and steadied myself with a hand on the stump, only to have my feet slide out from under me, leaving me lying flat on the ground on my stomach, arms wrapped around my tree stump, and the maul buried in the snow at my side. As I paused there in the snow or, rather, strewn across the slickening ice, contemplating my position, the log tilted over and hit me in the head before it fell to the ground and rolled down the hill and into the woods in a pointed little accent to my predicament. I checked to see if I still had all my fingers.

Now I was pissed—the perfect frame of mind to accomplish anything. It would be too disturbing to probe the reasons why I chose to continue. But I did.

I got to my feet, gingerly working my way back down the small hill to get another log and back up to set it on the tree stump. I took hold of the maul and once again positioned myself below the stump, ready for the kill. Having learned a bit of a lesson, and invoking my ski skills, I jammed my foot into the ice to gain a grip. My sneakers were wet, and my feet were freezing. That kick in the snow sent a blue streak of pain up through my legs. The music swelled. I lifted the maul over my shoulder, sucked in a breath, and brought it down on the log with a lusty war cry.

The head sank into the log about an inch. Barely a dent. Clearly not a split log. Too timid, I said to myself. I'll nail it this time. Raised the maul over my shoulder again, let out another battle cry, and brought the head down onto that log with the might of Thor. Nearly missed the log completely. The maul sliced off a sliver of bark along the side of the log. This was going to require a little more skill than I had imagined.

Clearly, a more aggressive approach was in order. I dug in my feet and measured my stroke to where I could halve the log. Then, this time, I took the handle of the maul and raised it directly overhead, arms stretched high. I prepared to bring down the maul with the wrath of a Barbarian, sucked in a deep breath, and felt the weight of the maul pulling me off balance, pulling my arms back. My feet slipped out from under me as I performed a half back flip into the snow. The miracle was that all my arms and legs were still connected. I got mad. I got up. I grabbed my maul and charged back to the stump. I raised that thing over my head again and, again, tumbled backward into the snow. I lay there, exhausted, foolish. Breathing heavily. I could feel my face grow crimson. I was cold. I was wet. My feet hurt. My arms hurt. My back hurt. Enough of this Paul Bunyan crap. It was then I understood how the Olympic hammer-throw event came into being. I grabbed the maul at the handle's end, twirled it one time and, with a shriek that would wake the devil himself, hurled the thing into the woods.

You can hear that scream echoing through the forest still.

I went in the house and called the firewood guy.

VI.

Brickhauser dropped the hose and growled, still staring up at the house.

OK, guys, let's go.

The ladders were put into place, and Brickhauser's guys climbed back up and set to work sealing the house and installing the bat doors.

Cesar and Guillermo were taking a well-deserved break, spread out on the grass under a tree that couldn't have offered much relief from the heat. They drank from a thermos that they passed back and forth, and Laura brought out a bunch of bottles of water. Guillermo took the first bottle and poured it over his head.

Then Laura and I stood in the driveway and watched the bat guys at their work for a few minutes and considered the shutterless, blotched and stained front of the house. No doubt about it, we were going to have to paint the outside.

So, Cesar, after you finish the inside, and after the bat guys are done, and when the bats are gone, we're gonna want you to paint the outside of the house.

No hay problema. What is the color? Same or different?

Well, first, how much would it cost? I'm not even sure why I asked.

All the house?

Yes, the whole thing. The outside.

OK. We do one coat of primer, two coats color, and the trim.

Right. How much? And how long will it take?

OK. I see and I tell you.

OK.

Later.

Later?

Sí, later. Now we paint the inside. Later I look and tell you the outside.

OK. Thank you.

Then he turned and pulled a phone out of his pocket. I think he was calling his retirement planner.

Brickhauser said as he was leaving, It's all sealed up, so keep everything closed for a couple of days. They can get through any kind of small hole. Couple of days, you should be all right.

How do we get in and out of the house? asked Laura. Will they come in the door when we open it?

Nah, just don't leave anything open. Keep the place closed up, but you can go in and out.

OK, Laura nodded. We'll keep everything closed up tight, she repeated the instructions solemnly.

A little later, I heard a scream from my office upstairs.

What's going on? As I ran to the room.

There was Laura shouting at poor Cesar, yelling, Close the window, close the window! Close it, close it! Shut the window!

Cesar was kneeling in a corner, painting the trim, sweat pouring over his body and down his face in the unrelenting, stifling heat. The nearby window was open to provide a modicum of comfort, a wisp of fresh air. In order to get the painting done, he'd had to remove the window air conditioner. It wasn't very effective on sweltering days, but it was better than nothing, and now it was disconnected entirely. The room was a sauna. It was hard for me to catch my breath, and I wasn't doing any painting.

Laura kept shouting, Close it! Close it! The bats! The bats!

Cesar was frozen (how ironic) in place, confused, not knowing what to do.

Laura, I said, calm down, calm down. There are no bats now. They won't be flying around until later. It's the middle of the day. Broad daylight. It's OK. It's OK.

It's not OK. We need to keep the windows closed! He said keep everything closed.

She crossed the room and slammed the window closed, then stared at the fresh white paint on her hands.

I'm sorry, she said more softly. The windows have to stay closed. We can't let the bats in.

Cesar nodded and went back to his work; the air conditioner sat lifeless in the middle of the floor.

It's stifling in here, I said. Cesar, you should stop for now. Put the air conditioner back in the window, and then go home. You can't work in here with the windows closed.

Has to dry. I paint the rest, then put the air conditioner back.

Look, it's too hot. *Muy caliente*. Go home. Come back tomorrow.

No, no. We paint. Finish this room today. Maybe the rest tomorrow. And I tell you about the outside.

I heard Laura closing windows in other rooms.

Hey, hey, I said when I found her in our bedroom. You know, there are screens on the windows. We can keep the windows open. The bats can't get through the screens.

He said they can get through any small hole.

Screens?

Any small hole.

Screens?

Any small hole. Besides, I'm not staying in here with bats banging into the screens. They might break through. We're keeping this place closed up tight until the bats are gone for good.

There was clearly no arguing with her on this point. The windows were closed and were going to stay closed. The air in the house, what there was of it, was still and oppressive.

Back in my office, Cesar and Guillermo were struggling to get the air conditioner back into the window. Laura stood in the doorway, on full anti-bat alert. She noticed where Cesar had opened one window a slight crack, obviously to allow him to breathe.

I'm sorry, Cesar, she said. We have to keep the windows closed so the bats can't get back in. I know it's hard. Why don't you finish up for the day? Come back tomorrow.

Sí.

He chattered instructions to Guillermo, and the two of them wrestled the air conditioner back into place. They turned it on and then left to wash up outside. I stood in front of the old air conditioner, running it full blast. In the face of the relentless heat and lack of air movement, it was only minimally effective. Just slightly cooling the room. It would take hours to really drop the temperature. Still, it was something.

We need to keep those windows closed. I mean it. We're not messing around with these bats.

Well, don't worry. I'm not going to open the window with the AC on, I said testily.

I mean everywhere.

Look, there are screens on the windows. Get a hold of yourself, will ya? You really ought to reconsider this.

OK. I've reconsidered. Now keep the windows closed.

Out on the driveway, Cesar and Guillermo dripping with sweat, were washing up with the garden hose. After washing paint from his hands and arms, Cesar just tilted the hose up and sprayed the water in his face. If it's possible, his face was wetter before he hosed it. They were nearly playing with the water now, just trying to cool off, not minding that their clothes were soaked.

After a few minutes, I went over to ask.

So what about the outside, Cesar? Can you do it? How much?

Sí. The outside. We can do it maybe next week.

How much?

Maybe four, five days.

I see. How much will that cost?

We do the primer, then two coats color and the trim.

Uh-huh. How much?

What color you want? Same or different?

I'm not sure. Probably the same. How much will it cost?

Cesar shouted in Spanish over to Guillermo, who shouted back.

Maybe five days, he said.

Yeah, and how much?

Next week, but we see the weather.

But I need to know how much it will cost, I said. What's your estimate?

He stared up at the house; up at the big, dirty blotches and discoloring where the shutters and beehives had been, nodding his head ever so slightly.

For you, maybe *finzintilliones dólares*.

OK, I said, resigned. Next week?

Sí. We finish the inside, and good weather and maybe five days next week. You tell me color.

They finished cleaning up, packed up the truck and were on their way. The day was coming to an end. The sun hung low in the sky. The sun was going down!

I looked to the skies. A little nervous. A little panicked, actually. I was bracing for an onslaught of hell-bent-on-destruction bats. I made a quick check of the grounds. Cars were in the garage, garage doors closed. Nothing else out. All quiet. I quickly strode to the front door with, for no real reason, my arms crossed over my head.

The door was locked.

Laura, Laura, I was screaming. Let me in! I'm at the door, let me in! Yo! Hey! Open up! Let me in!

What's going on? she said, opening the door a crack.

Hurry up, let me in. Close the door. It's getting dark. They'll be flying out of here soon.

We'd descended into completely irrational behavior.

OK, OK. Get in. Everything is closed up.

I surveyed the house, anyway. Room by room, window by window. I wouldn't admit to it, but I was as timid as Laura. I envisioned the long night and the coming bat assault in the morning. Angry bats in droves banging their little bat fists on the windows—need I say it—going batshit to get back in their house.

It's early, but what do you want to do for dinner?

Nothing. I'm not hungry. I'm just going to go upstairs and do some work.

You sure? There's some tuna if you just want to make a sandwich.

The house was so hot. Boxed-in hot.

No. I'm going upstairs. At least the office has an air conditioner. Come hang out in there. It'll be a little cooler.

No, I'm just going to watch TV or read my book. I'll turn on the fan and just try to get through the night.

She filled a plastic bag with ice from the freezer. Headgear.

Up in the office, I relished the relative coolness. The air conditioner had managed to lower the temperature to about 85, but it was still the coolest room in the house. I sat down at my computer and set to work with a nervous ear listening for the sound of the departing bat mob.

Time passed slowly. It wasn't quite dark yet, but the light was fading. It was right around bat time. The still air was broken only by the hum of the air conditioner and the clicking of fingers on keyboard. A clock ticked in the hall (I made that part up). And then—

Everything stopped.

The air conditioner went silent, the computer went dead, the imaginary clock halted.

Power out.

Great.

I went downstairs to find Laura sitting on the couch, bag of ice on her head, staring at the blank TV.

Power's out, I said.

She just looked at me.

I don't believe it. Can you believe it?

She stared,

No lights, no air, no fans, no TV. Wonderful. Just wonderful.

Then, out of nowhere, a tapping. Tap, tap. Tapping . . . tapping, tapping. On the roof, through the walls. Then harder, and harder, like stones falling, building to a rush.

Then a roar. Hail! It was hailing! Pieces of ice the size of golf balls were pummeling down on the house. Covering the deck. Coating the driveway. A torrent of stones. The house shook. We froze in place, hunched, cowering. It was frightening. It felt like the roof would cave in, the windows would break. And if the windows broke, the bats—

Oh my god! I yelled. It was all I could take. *Enough!* I cried out, my arms held wide, beseechingly.

HEAT, BATS, BEES, POWER, HAIL, SARCASM OF THE FIRST BORN! HOW MANY MORE PLAGUES, LORD?! I shouted, shaking my fist at the ceiling.

It was a lazy Saturday morning one spring. We were having coffee in the kitchen when Laura glanced out the window.

Look at that, she pointed smiling, a bunch of puppies rolling down the hill.

Sure enough, there were five, six little puffy balls of gray, rolling playfully down the hill in our backyard. Very cute. You couldn't help but smile.

I don't think they're dogs, though, I said. I think they might be, could be, foxes.

Really? They're so cute. Look at them just tumbling down the hill.

The whole bunch of them disappeared into the woods, just beyond the fieldstone wall that bordered our property.

Huh. Wow. Foxes, I said. Pretty cool.

Later that afternoon, I was looking out into the woods and saw some activity along the ground among the old fallen trees, branches and thick growth, the forest-bottom debris. Squinting into the woods, it looked like the fox pups were scampering about a long fallen, dead tree trunk. I couldn't make it out so well, so I went to get my binoculars.

There they were, as I peered through the lenses. The whole family of foxes grappling with sticks and nipping at each other and generally having a good old time there in the woods. They were a real curiosity, our own little commune with nature. Foxes.

I googled foxes. And everything to do with foxes. I searched and researched, studying everything I could find. I learned everything there was to know about foxes. I learned about their habitats, their hunting prowess, their feeding preferences, their sleeping schedules, their mating and breeding habits. I sorted through tons of pictures and behavioral studies. I learned about male foxes, female foxes, mature foxes, young foxes. I learned their favorite colors, their favorite TV shows, what they want to be when they grow up. I read and read, one article linked to another. I peered out the window with my binoculars, watching, studying. I learned everything. Everything. I learned what was undeniable. I learned that our foxes, weren't.

Coyotes.

We had a family of coyotes living in our backyard. No question about it.

So now I learned all about coyotes. All about those miserable coyotes. Males mate with a single female for years. They have pups in the early spring and remain with them until the fall, when the pups go out on their own—so coyotes are at least smart enough to ditch their kids before they turn into teenagers. The mother stays with the pups in their den most of the day, while Poppa goes out to hunt and bring back food, mostly small rodents. This raised so many questions. What did Momma do all day? I see no antenna, cable wire or satellite dish connected to that decaying old log. She probably doesn't even have Internet access so she can plop the kids down in front of some old YouTube video of Wiley Coyote. When Pops comes home, will she look at the meager chipmunk he lays at her feet and say How am I supposed to feed five kids with that? Go back out and grab a couple of rabbits or something.

A single pair of coyotes can occupy as much as ten square miles for their proprietary territory. Keep small dogs and cats away, as coyotes will often take them for food. Humans are generally safe. I liked that, generally.

I worried about the dog getting into a fight with a coyote. I worried about the coyotes coming over the wall to attack the house. I worried about coyotes taking over our land. I thought, Coyoteland—not gonna happen. I would stand up to these beasts, defend our home, stay strong in the face of danger. They've messed with the wrong exurbanite! Following the defensive tactics prescribed on the Internet, I opened the windows and banged pots together. That'll show 'em. After a determined bout of pot banging, I peered through my binoculars. There they were. Mr. and Mrs. John Q. Coyote and their family, dug in. Staring right back at me.

There was only one thing to do.

We greeted Brickhauser in the driveway as he pulled up and got out of his truck.

Whaddawegot?

Coyotes, said Laura.

Hmm, he grunted. Let's have a look.

We all went out back. I pointed, and Brickhauser led us to the wall, and I showed him where the coyotes were hanging out.

At first, I wasn't sure whether they were foxes or coyotes, I said, but I'm pretty sure they're coyotes.

Yeah, you can be sure OK.

Well, what are you going to do? asked Laura, a distinct nervousness in her voice.

Do you shoot them? I asked.

Brickhauser almost laughed—almost.

You can't shoot, 'em, he said.

Why not? We're not protecting coyotes, are we? I think you should shoot them.

Well, you might be able to shoot the first one, said an amused Brickhauser, but the rest ain't going to wait around after that. They'll scatter, then be back in their den a little while later. Besides, you can't fire a weapon here in a residential area.

Well, what are we going to do, trap them, poison them?

Nah. We're going to create an inhospitable environment. Have 'em move out all by themselves.

That doesn't sound very tough.

Maybe not, but it's effective.

What are you going to do then? I asked. Play loud polka music?

Brickhauser just tossed his head slightly and grunted. I'll be back tomorrow morning. We'll get those suckers out of there.

What do you mean tomorrow? said Laura. Can't you take care of it now?

Don't have what I need.

Well, what do you need?

See you in the morning.

Back to the truck. Gone.

I was obsessed. I watched the pack all through the day, binoculars fixed to my face. They kind of just seemed to play a little bit in the morning, then disappeared for most of the day. Nowhere to be seen. Still, I couldn't take my eyes off the log where I knew they were burrowed beneath. I was kind of afraid to turn my back, thinking I'd be attacked—or miss something. I wouldn't let the dog out there. I read more stuff on the Internet, looked at dozens of pictures, hoping, somehow, that they'd magically turn into foxes. The cute kind that avoided humans. Nope. They were coyotes. Nasty, dead-eyed, tail-dragging coyotes.

At dusk, they stirred. They appeared in my binocular lens. I armed myself and reluctantly, nervously, but purposefully, made my way out on the lawn and started banging my pots and pans. I watched through the evening and into the night, standing guard, making sure the coyotes didn't breach our property line, come across the wall and threaten the homeland. They weren't going to mess with me. I had cookware.

The next day I was up early and watched for hours as they milled about around their log—the five puppies, who seemed to have grown quite a bit in the last couple of days, and a larger one, presumably the mom. The even larger male was nowhere to be seen. I kept my pots and pans close at hand.

It was midmorning when Brickhauser showed up. I walked out to the truck as he pulled some stuff from the back: two jugs, a bag of rags and a long-handled shovel.

What's all this?

Come on.

We went around back, and Brickhauser purposefully strode across the lawn, dropped his stuff at the stone wall and climbed over. Then he slowed down and stealthily made his way into the woods, approaching the long dead log lying there near the edge of the woods. Home of the Fightin' Coyotes. There he stopped, crouched down a bit and put his finger to his lips, signaling me to be quiet. He carefully leaned over, then stooped down and peered into a hole under the log. He nodded to himself, tilted his head and peered in some more. If it was a horror movie, a great claw would have sprung out and grabbed him by the face, pulling him down into the dark nothingness of coyote hell. Nothing like that happened. Instead, Brickhauser stood up, then peered into the surrounding woods, studying the area, and turned his head to look in each direction.

He came back to where I stood, safe, well away from the wall.

Yep, they're in there. Sound asleep. I didn't see Daddy in there, though. He's probably out hunting.

What are we going to do? (We?)

Well, we're going to soak these rags in this ammonia. Then we stuff the rags into the den, and all around the area. (We?) Coyotes' sense of smell is a hundred times greater than ours. They're going to hate it. They'll vacate and won't come back.

That works?

Pretty good chance. I'll come by in a couple of days and see how we did.

So he pulled on some thick leather gloves and started soaking a bunch of the rags with the ammonia. Then he stuffed them back in the bag, which he threw over his shoulder, picked up the shovel, and said, Come on. Let's go.

Well, I can just wait here.

No no, come on, let's go.

We walked toward the stone wall. I lagged behind a little as Brickhauser scissored over the wall with ease. He turned back to look for me. I was moving slowly, nervously scanning the surrounding area, studying the woods, convinced I could see coyotes looming among the trees. I didn't—I don't think.

Hey, come on, he said in a loud whisper. What's going on?

I'm coming, I whispered back. Just want to make sure they don't surround us. I moved more quickly to catch up. I thought it might be better if I stood right beside Brickhauser. We paused quietly for a moment, just next to the entrance to the coyote den. I was terrified.

OK, said Brickhauser in a low voice, here we go. I'm going to put a bunch of these rags near the entrance to the den, he whispered. Should do the trick.

What do I do with this? I asked as he handed me the shovel.

You watch out for Poppa. If he comes back, hit him with it. Hard.

The next afternoon, there was a note taped to our front door in big block letters: COYOTES GONE. B.

VII.

Sensing movement in the room, I awoke from a light sleep. Laura was at the window.

What time is it? I asked, rubbing my eyes. It was still dark.

Late, early. Like four thirty.

What are you doing?

Seeing if the bats are coming back.

Is the power back on?

No.

You OK?

Shh.

What shh?

I'm trying to hear if there are bats.

I listened too.

I don't hear anything, I said.

Shh.

I'm going to try to fall back asleep. Come back to bed.

Shh.

OK. Wake me if anything happens. God, there's no air in here. Do you think we can open the windows now?

Absolutely not. They'll be coming back soon. No. Shh.

But there was no sleeping. I just lay there, sticky and uncomfortable in the heat, kicking at the bedding, tossing the pillow back and forth to the cool side. Waiting for bats, feeling sorry for us and our predicament. Maybe Jason was right those years ago. We should've stayed in The City. We weren't cut out for this crap.

Ooh. Ooh. Listen, said Laura. I hear something. There's something.

What? Is it the bats? What do you hear?

I got up and went to the window.

Hear that? she said. That tapping?

Yeah, maybe. I listened hard but wasn't sure.

She cocked her head at the window, trying to see the roof, but couldn't get an angle on it.

I think they're trying to get in the attic vents.

Ha! Bat doors, I said.

Hear them now? I can hear them. They're trying to get in. *Whhoof*, she shuddered.

Look, I said, pointing up and out across the lawn. You can see some flying toward the house. Watch, you'll see.

Oh my god. They're here. Trying to get in.

We backed off from the window and stood in the middle of the room, looking up at the ceiling. Hoping the attic above would hold firm. Listening. Hoping the bat doors would do their job.

I don't know how long we stood there, but I noticed that the sun had come up.

What now? I asked. Do you hear anything?

No. You?

No.

We stayed in place. What should we do?

I don't know. She stood with her arms wrapped around her.

Well, we can't just stand here. I'm going to put some clothes on and see what's going on outside. I'm bigger than a bat.

Be careful.

Call the electric company and see if they have an estimate on when the power will be back. This is nuts.

I ventured out into the morning heat, cautious, timid, with my head tucked into my shoulders.

They must be gone, I whispered to myself. Nothing here.

I walked all around the outside of the house, surveying the roofline, looking up at the attic vents with their mesh bat doors. All quiet, all still, nothing to see. I looked up in the trees. Nothing. Nothing anywhere.

Well, I said, out loud now, they must be gone. I felt my body release and straighten from having been crouched in cautiousness.

Back in the house, I told Laura all was clear.

Nothing going on out there. Not a thing. All clear. Show's over. I guess Brickhauser knew what he was doing.

Are you sure? Nothing?

Nope. Not a thing. All quiet. Not a bat in sight. Did you call the power company?

Yes. Nothing. No estimate when the power will be back.

Well, at least now we can open a few windows around here. Let some air in.

Oh no.

What?

Brickhauser said a couple of days. We're not opening anything. Let's not screw it up.

But it's broad daylight. There's nothing out there. Even if there was, they won't be back until later. Bats aren't going to be trying to fly into the house in the daytime. They're off at some other bat B&B, snoring away, dreaming of a big all-you-can-eat breakfast tonight—not to mention house hunting. They've got places to go, things to do. Stop being crazy.

I'm not being crazy. He said a couple of days, and we're not taking any chances. They're out. We're not letting them back in.

Oh my god. I can't take this anymore. Oh look, here's Cesar. I'm surprised he's not driving up in a limo.

Laura went out to meet him in the driveway. Cesar, she waved, walking over to greet him. Remember, we can't open the windows. The windows have to stay closed. Bats. No windows.

I'm not sure, but I think Cesar was about to cry.

I really couldn't stay in the house any longer. The power was still out, I couldn't get any work done, and I was fed up with managing our wildlife foundation. Besides, I had to get out of the heat before I burst into flames and was consumed by the bat gods.

Look, I said to Laura, you can put all the ice on your head you want. I've got to find a place where I can get some work done, and if the power's not back today, we're getting a hotel room for the night.

We can't leave Maggie here by herself.

I'll find a place that takes pets.

Just getting into the car was a relief. Only a few minutes away, in town, everything was normal. It was amazing. People going about their business, no power outage, no panic. Civilization. I found myself a seat at Starbucks and plugged in my computer, powered up my phone, and got a *grande* ice coffee. The room was cool; the coffee was cool; my computer was on. Even the bathroom worked. Modern plumbing! This was living. I started to run through emails, but then got sidetracked—the sports pages, newspaper columns, Facebook, YouTube, TV excerpts—everything, anything, but work. Time passed, but I was enjoying myself. I'd have felt self-conscious taking up a seat without ordering anything, so I was on my fourth cup of coffee. Well, two ice coffees and two caramel Frappuccinos. By this time, my heart was racing. I was getting fidgety, getting nuts actually. I was thinking faster, typing faster, heading to the bathroom faster. My skin was crawling. Caffeine-induced chaos.

Then I remembered. Oh jeez. Damn. My mind was racing, 'cause I needed to get a hotel room for the night, maybe more—a hotel room, one that took dogs, pets, Maggie—hotel room for later for tonight with electricity, and cool, with air-conditioning, and where we could stay until the power came on, when we could go back home. And how come the whole damn town had power except us, and what the hell was going on with the bats and everything, and now we had to get the front of the house painted 'cause of the bees' nests. And god, it was going to cost a fortune, and I can't believe we had all those bats to begin with, and what the hell were we doing living in the country anyway, with all the damn trees and bats and bees and all the people going in and out. And . . . oh yeah, I better find a hotel room for tonight that takes pets.

I was a little on edge.

OK. First things first. I placed my hands purposefully on the table in front of me and gained control of myself. Deep breath. I needed to find a hotel room for the night—one that would allow our girl, Maggie, an eighty-pound chocolate lab who, quite frankly, could stand to lose a few pounds.

I did an online search of local hotels, looking for one that accepted dogs. None of the chains took pets, but a little local motel was listed as pet friendly.

Hi. I need a room for tonight. King bed. One night, possibly two, or until we get our power back. Well, what do you have available? Two queens will do. How much?

Really. OK, and I want to confirm you allow pets. Yes. A dog. Well, how big do you allow? Oh, I guess she's about twenty pounds. I'm not actually sure, but something like that. When's check-in time? OK. Thanks.

I called Laura.

It's me. Power on yet? Jeez. OK, I got a room for tonight. That place Twin Pines, up Route 24. Yes, they allow pets. What's going on there? Oh? When's he coming back? You sure? OK. Look, if anyone asks, Maggie weighs about twenty pounds. I know, I know. Well, here's the plan. I'll drive up there and check-in this afternoon, so we don't have to stop at the desk later. I'll get the keys, then, when we go over there later, one of us will distract the clerk while the other sneaks Maggie past the desk and into the room. Of course it will work. Well, we'll make it work. Don't worry about it. Of course it's clean. Three stars. (I lied.) Triple A. (I lied.)

The thing about having a dog in the woods, especially a hunting dog, is that they like to go after critters. Now there's a word I never thought I'd utter.

Like the night I wasn't feeling quite myself. I'd gone up to bed early. The rest of them were down in the family room watching TV. Even though I hadn't been feeling well, I was lying in bed in that half consciousness between sleep and awake, totally relaxed, almost euphoric. Actually feeling pretty good, finally, after a rough day. Alone in the dark, floating, blissful.

And then all hell broke loose. I shook myself awake and realized that the ruckus below had actually started several minutes before it made its way through the darkness into my scull and raised my awareness. I heard panicked yelling as I roused from my stupor. The boys were yelling; Laura was screaming; the dog was barking frantically. A cacophony. For reasons I can't explain, calliope music streamed through my mind. I felt the swirl of chaos all around, emanating from the room below, while the circus music blared on. Then I heard Laura calling my name. With urgency. Loudly. Really loudly. Screaming.

I pulled on my jeans, annoyed that my reverie had been interrupted. Couldn't they handle anything themselves?

I descended the stairs into mayhem. The boys were shouting; Laura was screaming at the dog; the dog was yelping with excitement. I noticed my eyes stinging and tearing—and the unmistakable, overwhelming, nausea-inducing, entirely too-close-at-hand stench of skunk.

Maggie had captured a skunk and proudly deposited her injured prey on the back deck. The skunk did what skunks do. The dog was running around in a heightened state of excitement, panic, and discomfort, resulting in loud and incessant barking the likes of which we'd never heard. The boys, running around the backyard in circles in the dark, tried to corral Maggie by yelling at her to calm down and calling to her, Get over here, but were having little success. It was hard to know whether Maggie was completely agitated or thought the whole thing was a game of tag that she was winning. Meanwhile, Laura was standing at the open doors to the deck, uncontrollably screaming a stream of loosely connected words and names at the top of her lungs: *MAGGIE BOYS STEVE MAGGIE JASON STEVE STEVEN GET DOWN HERE MATT GET OVER HERE MAGGIE SKUNK SKUNK IT'S A SKUNK OH MY GOD MAGGIE MAGGIE GET OVER HERE STOP STOP MAGGIE COME COME OH MY GOD BOYS STEVE GET HOLD OF MAGGIE OH GOD.*

Neither Laura nor the boys nor Maggie nor the gods themselves seemed able to bring things to order. I stood in the middle of the family room, immersed in the chaos around me, the calliope reverberating in my head.

The days that followed were all skunk, all stink, all the time. Everything, I mean everything, stunk from skunk. We tried every possible measure to rid the house of the smell. But it was an intractable living thing. It was an evil being, risen from the depths of hell to cast its smelly shadow over the earth. It was everywhere—in the house, in our clothes, in our hair, in our skin. Skunk, skunk, skunk. We bathed the dog in every shampoo we could find, shampoos of every color, scent and viscosity. We had recommendations from the vet, friends and neighbors, the Internet. Nothing worked. Poor Maggie stunk to high heaven. No one wanted to be near her. The poor sweet dog ached to be petted, but no one would touch her. We'd get more skunk on us. Finally, we took to bathing her in tomato juice, tomato soup, tomato sauce. Between the shampoo and the tomato juice, she was turning into a canine pizza.

But it wasn't just Maggie. We all smelled. We all stunk from skunk. The boys didn't want to go to school because the other kids kept far away from them. We were all so self-conscious. I felt like we were leaving a little trail of noxious fumes behind us. We walked around the house smelling our clothes and making sour faces. When we parked our cars in a parking lot we didn't have to remember where they were. We just sniffed the air and followed the stench. We were enveloped in a blanket of skunk. We reeked. Surely the town would soon issue a decree banishing us to Devil's Island.

I don't know how long it lasted. Days. Weeks. Months? One day we just noticed that the smell was gone. In town, people stopped crossing the street to avoid us. At school, kids sat next to the boys again. We could take Maggie to the park again without the other dog owners scurrying for cover.

We bought new cars.

It's funny how humans adapt to their environment. After years of living in the woods and our various brushes with the great outdoors, we began to take things more in stride.

There was the evening I went to take out the trash, to deposit it in the large garbage can we keep in the garage. As I was stuffing the bag into the container, I noticed something on the floor. I grabbed a shovel and set to the task.

A short while later, I went back into the house, where Laura looked up from the TV.

What was going on out there, she asked.

Hmm?

Banging, clanging. All that ruckus. What was going on out there?

Snake, I said matter-of-factly.

And we both went back to watching TV.

VIII.

It's only about fifteen minutes up to Twin Pines, an old motel along a secondary two-lane highway outside of town. Two wings of rooms with a central office. Maybe thirty rooms total. Two big pine trees out front. I wanted to check out the place and register ahead of time. There was a skinny young guy at the desk, tousled hair, thick black-rimmed glasses and a noticeably oversized plastic watch.

Hi there.

Hi. I called earlier to reserve a room?

You are?

Bowman.

Yes. I have you right here.

Good. And pet friendly, right.

Yes. We allow small pets. Cats and dogs under twenty pounds.

I guess she's about twenty pounds. I never actually weighed her, I said with a chuckle. You know, it's not like she's watching her weight or anything.

Just so it's a small dog.

Right. No problem. I could feel the big fake smile spreading across my face.

OK. Will that be cash or credit?

Um, credit. The place was a mid-twentieth-century remnant. He carefully took my credit card and slid it through the machine as if afraid he was going to break it.

There you go. Just sign my copy right there, and you can sign-in right here. He pointed to a line in an old-fashioned manual ledger.

There you go.

How many keys?

Two, please.

There you go. Pet-friendly number 17. He handed me two old classic keys attached to big blue plastic keychains with the room number. The plastic key chains bore the name and address of the motel: If found return to Twin Pines.

And we have coffee here in the lobby at 6:00 a.m. Free.

Oh, and I can get the room again tomorrow night if I need to? We don't have power.

No problem. So how long have you been out?

Three days now. They don't know when it will be back.

That's rough. Well, enjoy your stay.

Thanks.

I went down a long hallway to find the room, thinking there was no way we were going to get Maggie past that desk without someone seeing her. I thought maybe I could throw a hood over the clerk's head and pretend it was just a gag. That's exactly how I would phrase it:

Well, Your Honor, it was just a gag.

The room was everything you'd expect. Oh, this was going to go over well. Nostalgic roadside-motel yuk. Drab green and brown everything. Worn rug, frayed curtains, dark. Was it possible that with all the lamps turned on, the shadows made it even darker? The two double (not queen) lumpy-looking beds each had a single, equally lumpy-looking pillow, and they were covered by faded red-floral bedspreads. There was an old scratched-up wood dresser with a TV. Next to the dresser was a small desk with a phone and some stationary with a picture of the two pines. There was a small bathroom with a small tub that might have been the perfect size for, say, soaking the soles of your feet. There was a small sink, good for nothing that came to mind. Everything was small. It was quite a marvel of engineering, demonstrating the ability to fit in every essential thing in the least amount of space. A semi-modern marvel. A pair of white, sort of, towels hung loosely from a worn silver rack over the toilet, but I swear you could see through them. A miniature bar of soap lay at the sink's edge, in a wrapper that would surely disintegrate if it was touched. The toilet had a clean paper band around the seat, but when you lifted the lid you could see that the porcelain on the bottom was worn and scratched with black stains. The windows looked out onto the road through the pine trees, barely visible through the filthy screens. A constant rattle came from the futilely blowing air conditioner stuck through the wall under the window.

Laura was going to love it.

I stood in front of the bathroom mirror and tried out lines for when she first walked in:

Well, this is going to be quite an adventure!

Cozy, huh?

Boy, a real classic.

Mmm. Just the place for a romantic getaway.

Man, they sure don't make 'em like this anymore.

Do you want to shower first?

I'll take the side by the door.

Or, finally, You know, the back seat of the car is pretty comfy.

Back at home, things were eerily quiet. No trucks in the driveway, no one working. I saw the house was still sealed up, no air conditioner running. The house stood blotched, stained, pocked, shutterless and silent. A real mess, in dire need of a board-certified house-front dermatologist.

This is it, I thought as I went through the front door.

Laura, I called, let's get packed up. Come on. Let's get Maggie and get the hell out of here until the power comes back. This is nuts.

She came into the kitchen holding a bag of ice on her head. I couldn't even laugh any more.

OK. They take dogs, right?

Yep. Let's go.

How long should I pack for?

Just a day or two. If we need anything, we'll come back and get it. Come on. Let's get the hell out of here.

All right. Let me just get some stuff together.

I'll get Maggie's food and bowls. And her leash.

Maggie didn't really need the leash, but I figured I could use it to keep Laura from running out of the motel room once she saw it.

We loaded up the car, and Maggie jumped in with a level of enthusiasm clearly out of proportion to the venture.

Thank god, said Laura. I don't think I could stay in that house for another second. Look at me, I'm a mess. I can't wait to take a good shower.

I didn't say a thing.

We headed out of the driveway and started up the lane with a little remorse, like we were deserting a sinking ship, and a modicum of optimism, like we were getting off a sinking ship. In the rearview mirror, I could see the house, looking dilapidated in need of new paint, sealed up like a tomb, and we hoped, by now, bat free.

Two-thirds of the way up the lane, I hit the brakes. There was a huge power-company truck sprawled across the roadway, four huge stanchions at the corners, splayed out, dug into the ground, and holding up a basket contraption with a power-company guy working on the lines overhead. The truck was dug in. Nothing was getting past it, in or out of that lane.

I stared through the windshield, trying to understand the situation before me. We clearly weren't going anywhere. Maggie started whimpering. No, sorry. It was Laura.

I got out of the car and went to speak to the guy in the truck.

Hey—what's going on?

Working on the power lines.

You mean for our house? The house down this lane?

That you down there? Yeah. You should be getting your power back.

When?

About twenty minutes, I guess.

Really?

Yeah, really. You're not going to be able to get out of here for about a half hour though. Can't move this rig until he's done up there.

Oh no. No problem. Let him get his work done. No problem at all. I'm just going to back up right back down that lane. Thanks. That's great. Thanks.

What's going on, Laura asked as I went back to the car, a spring in my step.

I was so excited, I could barely spit it out.

We're going to have power in about twenty minutes!

Really?

Yes. Really!

Dancing in the lane! Unmitigated joy! I kneeled in the roadway and gave thanks to the deities—all of them. I chanted psalms and raised my arms shouting Hallelujah! Laura wept. I swore to be a better man and resolved not to eat red meat for a month. I considered offering Jason as a sacrifice to give thanks.

I started up the car and began backing back down the lane. Down the hill and around the bend . . . and into the ditch.

IX.

The summer of the bats was years ago, long ago. A memory.

Now I sit here on a beautiful Sunday afternoon in October. The fire's dancing. The boys are over and the game is on. Maggie is curled up next to me on the couch, her head resting in my lap. The chips are crispy, the salsa is spicy and the beer is cold. Laura is lining shelves somewhere.

Outside, the woods are bright with the colors of fall, the leaves forming a vivid canopy over the lane in gold, orange and yellow. The air is sweet with the scent of autumn.

We're happy and comfortable in our home, nestled in our woods, settled in our town.

Suddenly, the serenity is broken.

Oh my god! screams Laura, running into the room in a panic, Look!

Jeez, I breathe, what is that? Wide-eyed staring through the den doors across the back lawn.

It . . . It's . . .

Holy crap. It's a bear!

ACKNOWLEDGMENTS

In our house, at the bottom of a stairway is a wall hanging—a sign, actually—in colorful big-block letters. It says simply LAUGH. That is the story of our household. It can be a tough room, and you've got to be able to take it as well as dish it out. Can you top this one-upmanship is sport. Even the occasional harsh word soon devolves into a recurring joke, available to be pulled out even years later as circumstances and the need for ridicule demand. But we wouldn't have it any other way. That's how it's always been in our house, and an unsurprising result is *Summer of the Bats*.

If you've arrived at this page after reading the book, I thank you and hope you've had a good time. If you're contemplating beginning, go ahead and take a shot. I think you'll enjoy it—and thank you for coming this far.

My thanks to Lynne Bloom, Alex Bloom and Diane Pershing for reading early drafts and sharing their comments and suggestions. I so appreciate the generous gift of their time, and the finished work is better for their contributions.

My thanks, as well, to editor extraordinaire Annie Jo Smith, who "got it" and patiently worked with a newbie to create a much better final work than would have otherwise been possible. Annie's sharp pen and keen insights were invaluable, creating clarity out of confusion and suggesting a better approach when I tried to make the wrong one do. And finally, so much thanks to my family, Lynne, Alex and Zack, who bring laughter to the world, tolerate my quirks, and surround me and each other with love and support. They make life joyous.

ABOUT THE AUTHOR

Stu Bloom and his wife, Lynne, enjoy their home near the beach in Fairfield, Connecticut. Among the many things Stu would like to do are play the guitar, speak Mandarin, and hang a picture at the right height on the first try.